FAMILY
AND
NATION

ALSO BY DANIEL PATRICK MOYNIHAN

Loyalties

*Counting Our Blessings: Reflections on the
Future of America*

A Dangerous Place

Ethnicity: Theory and Experience
(Editor, with Nathan Glazer)

Coping: Essays on the Practice of Government

The Politics of a Guaranteed Income

On Equality of Educational Opportunity
(Editor, with Frederick Mosteller)

*On Understanding Poverty: Perspectives from
the Social Sciences* (Editor)

Toward a National Urban Policy (Editor)

*Maximum Feasible Misunderstanding:
Community Action in the War on Poverty*

*The Defenses of Freedom: The Public Papers
of Arthur J. Goldberg* (Editor)

*Beyond the Melting Pot: The Negroes,
Puerto Ricans, Jews, Italians, and Irish
in New York City* (with Nathan Glazer)

DANIEL

PATRICK

MOYNIHAN

FAMILY AND NATION

The Godkin Lectures
Harvard University

HARCOURT

BRACE

JOVANOVICH,

PUBLISHERS

San Diego   New York   London

HBJ

Copyright © 1986 by Daniel Patrick Moynihan

Library of Congress Cataloging in Publication Data

Moynihan, Daniel P. (Daniel Patrick), 1927–
    Family and nation.

    (The Godkin lectures; 1985)
    Includes index.
    1. Family policy—United States—
Addresses, essays, lectures.
2. Family—United States—
Addresses, essays, lectures.
3. Problem families—United States—
Addresses, essays, lectures.
I. Title.   II. Series.
HV699.M67   1986   362.8'2'0973   85-27041
ISBN 0-15-130143-3

Designed by Michael Farmer
Printed in the United States of America
First edition
A B C D E

For

Theodore H. White

at Seventy

CONTENTS

FOREWORD

The Godkin Lectureship was established at Harvard University in 1903 by friends of Edwin Lawrence Godkin, editor and founder of the *Nation*. The lecturer is asked to speak on "The Essentials of Free Government and the Duties of the Citizen. . . ." When invited to give the lectures in 1985, I chose the subject "Family and Nation." For my part this was a return to a subject I had touched upon some twenty years earlier, but in the changed context brought on by what Samuel H. Preston, in the 1984 Presidential Address to the Population Association of America, termed "the earthquake that shuddered through the American family in the past twenty years."

The essays begin at the time the earthquake began and for a stretch will strike the reader almost as narrative. Might I then take this occasion to offer assurances that it is not at all my purpose to return to earlier controversies. An account of the lectures, given in April at the John F. Kennedy School of Government, appeared in the *Economist*. Under the heading "Children in Poverty, America's Disgrace," the article began by noting that when I first raised the subject of family breakup, during the Johnson administration in the 1960s, I "got a bloody nose." So I did. It wasn't my first and doesn't in the least concern me. What *does* engage me is the continued hope that as a polity we might a little better learn the uses of social science. Such uses are limited. There isn't a great deal *of* social science. Some argue there is none. I don't. To the contrary I have contended there are "modes of anticipation," including social science, that can be helpful and should be attended to. Social policy must flow from social values; social science never creates such values. Yet if attended to, it can help somewhat, at some times, to secure them. My purpose in narrating certain events is to point to moments when we might have done this, and did not. In this sense there are two subjects in these essays, and this ought not to be left to the reader to puzzle out.

In years past I have had the honor to give the Phi Beta Kappa Oration at Harvard College, then the Freshman Lecture, later the Commencement Address to the whole of the university. Now, having been appointed Godkin Lecturer for 1984–85, I have received about all that is in the gift of the university, and a sometime professor of government can only express a baffled but abounding gratitude.

Daniel Patrick Moynihan
Pindars Corners, New York
May 26, 1985

CHAPTER ONE

The Moment Lost

IN 1965 I published in *America* an article exceptional for its innocence but not unusual for its time. The United States, I wrote, seemed on the verge of adopting a national policy directed to the quality and stability of American family life. It would mean an extraordinary break with the past. This could be the central event of a new era of social legislation.

In the preceding months, I continued, the legislative agenda of the New Deal had finally been completed— nearly a quarter century after the effort began. The reason for the delay had been simple enough: the program had lost its majority in Congress in 1938 and had not won it back until 1964. But with that return, bills were passed "one-two-three-four." I cited the Elementary and Secondary Education Act, which was less of an event than we thought at the time, and Medicare, which was considerably more. With the elementals of social provision behind us and the goals set forth by the Employment Act of 1946 closer to reality than ever before—such was the seeming mastery of the economists of the age—we could and now would turn to a new complex of concerns centering on the well-being of families.

The article, if innocent, was not wholly naive, and it can be reread with some profit. The quality and decency of life in the United States, I contended, were incomparably greater than in years past. And yet there was a segment of our population whose lives had somehow not been touched by the general success, save to the extent they had fallen even further behind. Increasingly, family structure defined this population. It could be that the seeming anomaly was nothing of the sort but rather a process. It was, I thought, entirely possible that many of the processes that were producing prosperity were also producing much of our poverty; it might be that both sets of problems were in fact part of a single phenomenon: the pathology of postindustrial society. It was to this continuum of issues, or so it seemed to me, that the next period of social-policy making in the United States should address itself.

Brave new world! What deeds this challenge would summon forth! In truth, I opined, "one could hardly ask a more agreeable challenge." The GNP was bulging, and the receptivity to new ideas in Washington never greater. Richard N. Goodwin, still then of the White House staff, had recently spoken of the challenge of a great society that looked beyond the prospects of abundance to the problems of abundance. There was a restlessness in Washington; the President had set moving a series of task forces to develop a new agenda for the nation.

It was here the possibility of a national family policy most clearly emerged: American social policy until then had been directed toward the individual. The individual had been our primary unit of measurement: men, women, children, all lumped together. Our employment statistics counted as equally unemployed a father of nine, a housewife coming back into the labor market in her forties, and a teenager looking for a part-time job after school. The minimum wage required by law to be paid to any of these persons was exactly the same. If they should somehow have the same level of earnings, which would have been easy enough, and were to lose their jobs, the amount of unemployment insurance paid to each would have been exactly the same. American arrangements pertained to the individual, and only in the rarest circumstances did they define the family as the relevant unit.

This was a pattern almost uniquely American. Most of the industrial democracies of the world had adopted a wide range of social programs designed specifically to support the stability and viability of the family.

The most common provision was the family allowance, an automatic income supplement based on the number of children in a family. As a senator, John F. Kennedy had joined Senator Richard L. Neuberger of Oregon in proposing a federal study of family allowances in Canada, which Neuberger had encountered whilst working on the Alcan Highway during the Second World War. But nothing came of the proposal, and the subject did not much interest Kennedy as President. In 1962 he sent a message to Congress on public welfare programs that began with this sufficiently complacent proposition: "Few nations do more than the United States to assist their least fortunate

5

citizens—to make certain that no child, no elderly or hand-icapped citizen, no family in any circumstances in any State, is left without the essential needs for a decent and healthy existence."

If the young President had a complaint, it was that in "too few nations" were people "aware of the progressive strides this country has taken in demonstrating the humanitarian side of freedom." In the struggle for the hearts and minds of men, social welfare was to be advanced, or at very least advertised. The message did declare that welfare programs "must stress the integrity and preservation of the family unit" and contribute "to the attack on dependency, juvenile delinquency, family breakdown, illegitimacy, ill health and disability." But the sum of the particulars was to extend the then-temporary measure providing Aid to Families with Dependent Children (AFDC) benefits to families with an unemployed parent, which was to say two-parent families, and to provide federal matching grants to train more skilled personnel, especially social workers. Kennedy's social legislation, or rather his occasional pronouncements on the subject, was written by aides more than a little concerned that he not sound too Catholic, and "family" was one of those issues bishops would go on about. Hence the welfare message was a product of the bureaucracy which addressed that issue, when it did, more in terms of social work than of social legislation. The profession of social work had by then acquired a strong therapeutic bent in which family problems were seen as symptomatic of individual dysfunction to be treated individually or, at most, in the discrete unit of the family itself.

Nothing approaching family policy was considered in these years.

In the *America* article I speculated about our seeming aversion to the subject. To state that it was in the tradition of American individualism did not answer the question but merely restated it. I touched on Nathan Glazer's suggestion that there was suspicion that "the family structure of the European middle class produced personalities that were peculiarly susceptible to Fascist and Nazi ideologies. . . ." (Years later, in 1985, Laura Gellott, with admirable candor would write in *Commonweal* "Catholic corporate theory has, of course, been put to . . . dismal uses; most notably its flirtation with facism in 1930s Europe.") At some level of awareness, following the Second World War the "bourgeois family" had become politically suspect in the intellectual circles where a good deal of social thinking began.

There was, in any event, a great variety of family modes in America, an aftermath of immigration. The correlation between family cohesion and the general measures of economic and social achievement was high. (The educational attainments of Chinese- and Japanese-Americans had emerged with striking clarity in the 1960 census.) Yet apart from anthropology, there had been little systematic enquiry into family matters. There was a coherent body of Catholic "teaching" on the subject, significant because it was so at odds with prevailing economic doctrine (the family wage, for example, as against the market-determined price of labor), and there was an abundance of rhetorical piety and honest belief. But few facts.

Indeed at times it could appear that the family was the object of attack. What, after all, was the AFDC program but a family allowance for *broken* families? Generally speaking, one became eligible by dissolving a family or by not forming one. The French would think such an arrangement bizarre. I might better have written that Canadians would; but whether persuasive or not, the point was probably correct.

At the time the *America* article appeared, I had just finished four years in the Department of Labor, years in which the federal manpower-training and antipoverty programs began. Early on I had sensed, and now reported, the disparate impact such programs seemed to have on male, as against female, opportunity. Visiting a training site, one would encounter men on a dim shop floor banging away at automobile fenders, women in fluorescent-lit classrooms learning to operate business machines. The respective employment prospects of the two sex-defined occupations were clear enough. This pattern carried over into at least some of the poverty programs. In Project Head Start—one of the most promising efforts to bring hope to slum children—we were even so paying women (qualified, professional women, to be sure) up to $9.20 an hour to look after the children of men who couldn't make $1.50 an hour. Even so, these were not quite conventional thoughts, and soon sex-defined biases would routinely be assumed to favor males against females. But that was not universally so in 1965, and is not now, and in 1965 it was possible to say so without thought of giving offense.

My summation was equally guileless.

From the wild Irish slums of the nineteenth century eastern seaboard, to the riot-torn suburbs of Los Angeles, there is one unmistakable lesson in American history: a community that allows a large number of young men to grow up in broken families, dominated by women, never acquiring any stable relationship to male authority, never acquiring any set of rational expectations about the future—that community asks for and gets chaos. Crime, violence, unrest, disorder—most particularly the furious, unrestrained lashing out at the whole social structure—that is not only to be expected; it is very near to inevitable. And it is richly deserved.

Clearly, single-parent households can be a better, more healthful, more stable environment for children than the frequently violent, tortured alternative that leads to family breakdown in the first place. And yet as an ecological proposition the passage is defensible.

The unemployment rate for adult black males was then 9.2 percent, more than twice that of whites. (Twenty years later these rates have nearly doubled for both groups.) These were the very men we were expecting to rear stable, orderly, well-behaved children, and to do so in some of the worst urban housing in the Western world.

We were expecting the impossible, that much was clear to me, and we would end up with an impossible situation unless we addressed ourselves to the issue of what it takes for a working man to raise a family in an American city, and then saw to it that this was available. This was "The Case for a Family Policy," the title of the article.

I had precious little idea as to what a family policy would amount to but had in mind the example of the Employment Act of 1946. All that this legislation actually did was to create the Council of Economic Advisors. Yet it had had far greater impact than any "jobs bill." It had declared a *national policy*. The bill as first drafted had the title Full Employment Act. In the end Congress had opted for a more modest goal, declaring it to be the federal government's policy and responsibility "to use all practicable means" to promote "useful employment opportunities" for all those able, willing, and seeking to work. Other, not inconsistent goals were added. Thus there began the *Economic Report of the President*. Whatever happened to employment—when it rose, when it fell, for whom—we would thereafter know. (Consider that the Great Depression of the 1930s was never really recorded in American statistics. At that time employment was measured in the census, taken every ten years in the spring of the year. In the spring of 1930 there was not yet much unemployment, in the spring of 1940 the worst was well past.) The mere declaration of policy was an event; it marked acceptance of a social responsibility that had not been clear, that indeed had been much disputed. The less specific the legislation the more chances of its having influence, and this appeared to have been the case.

And so I had a model. In itself, I wrote in 1965, a national family policy did not need to be more complex than the provisions outlined in the Employment Act. The point was not what answers were provided, but what questions were posed. The Employment Act said nothing about how to achieve "useful employment opportunities" but rather declared that the national government should be continuously concerned that there were such. It would be enough for a national family policy to declare that the American government sought to promote the stability and well-being of the American family; that the social programs of the federal government would be formulated and administered with this object in mind; and finally that the President, or some person designated by him, would report to the Congress on the condition of the American family in all its many facets—not of *the* American family, for there is as yet no such thing, but rather of the great range of American family modes in terms of regions, national origins, and economic status.

Taxation appeared to be a good example of an area of government policy in which a general pronouncement would have considerable specific relevance. General impressions to the contrary, I contended that during the postwar period indirect taxes, which bear heaviest on the families of the poor, had risen as a proportion of all tax receipts. Most importantly, the value of the personal exemption in the income tax had steadily eroded since it had last been fixed, at $600, in 1948. The provision exempts from taxable income a fixed amount for each family member, the only feature of the tax system making allowance for the cost of raising children. President Kennedy had proposed a considerable tax cut, enacted in 1964, but the personal exemption had remained at its 1948 level. Tax policy was not the least affected by family considerations, for there was no family policy.

Some while later, in 1968, in an introduction to a paperback edition of Alva Myrdal's *Nation and Family* (first published in 1941), I would contend that "in the nature of modern industrial society no government, however firm might be its wish, can avoid having policies that profoundly influence family relationships. This is not to be avoided. The only option is whether these will be purposeful, intended policies or whether they will be residual, derivative, in a sense, concealed ones." I had come to this view by 1965 and presented it with considerable optimism.

Fifteen years later, again in *America*, I returned to the subject in a wholly different mood. My text was taken from an address given early in 1980 to a meeting of the Catholic League for Religious and Civil Rights in New York City, an organization founded by John LaFarge in 1934.

I went over the efforts, my own included, of the previous fifteen years to put in place something like a family policy and concluded that we had failed and, beyond failure, had all but forfeited any chance ever of success. It appeared to me that the difficulties I had touched upon in the 1965 article in *America* had proven decisive and would continue to prove so, only with the list lengthened. In the book *Interracial Justice,* subtitled *A Study of the Catholic Doctrine of Race Relations,* LaFarge, in 1937, set forth what appeared to me as the basic dictum: "deprivation is in itself unhealthful, and . . . it is our duty to combat it. . . . The right to economic security attaches *primarily* to the family, as the primary unit of society, and to the individual in his relation to the family." (His emphasis.) We were now at the wearied, mildly recriminatory end of a long period of "liberal" experimentation and change, and not much of anything *had* changed concerning the issues I had raised with such high hopes fifteen years earlier. American liberalism seemingly could not find a use for the social doctrine represented by LaFarge, a doctrine with which more traditional American progressivism is at best uneasy and of which is at worst deeply suspicious. Still, it seemed plain enough to me, if not so much as a matter of doctrine then of evidence. There is Freud's dictum: "Anatomy is destiny." So also of social structure. There can be, there is, no equality of social condition between groups, or generations, without some equivalence of social structure, for good or ill. It is easy to ignore or to deny this. Those who do are simply not equipped for the work and would do well to look for a less determinist field. Further, they *ought*. Georges Bernanos put it thus: "The worst, the most corrupting lies are problems poorly stated."

Between 1965 and 1980 I had been much involved with the effort to change the welfare system, in response not least to the way the welfare system had changed. (In the earliest period, dating from 1937, half the children receiving assistance from the Aid to Dependent Children [ADC] program had one or both parents dead. By the early 1940s the proportion had dropped below one-quarter. By the early 1980s only a handful of welfare families were needy because of a deceased husband. In nearly half of such families there had never been a husband.) The welfare reform movement—it was called reform because of the near-universal assumption that it was causing more difficulties than it was resolving—did yield one significant achievement.

The Family Assistance Plan proposed by President Nixon in 1969 did in the end produce the Supplemental Security Income (SSI) Program, a guaranteed income for the aged, the blind, and the disabled.

But that was my tale. The Family Assistance Plan had been devised first and foremost to provide a guaranteed income for children and for families with children. In the end, the only persons left out were children and families with children.

This was disappointing; and yet legislation comes when it will. The Supplemental Security Income Program was no small achievement. It was not what we had failed to do for children during that interval but what we had done to them that occasioned the near-embittered tone of this second *America* article. In 1965 it was possible to look to a future in which social policy would attempt to do more for children. Fifteen years later, in 1980, it was necessary to acknowledge that in fact social provision had been cut back, and sharply.

I was then, 1980, chairman of the Subcommittee on Public Assistance of the Senate Committee on Finance. We had recently held hearings on the prospects—dim—of further welfare reform. (Aid to the aged, the blind, the disabled, is as much a form of public assistance as aid to dependent children.) Few national organizations had chosen to appear; but a fair number of academics—especially now economists—continued their interest in the subject, and the testimony we took was grim enough. The principal point made to us was that owing to inflation, the provision for dependent children had been sharply reduced in the previous decade. Seemingly no one cared. Importantly, no one protested.

(To bring the data up to the present, from 1970 to 1985 maximum AFDC benefits for a four-person family declined 33 percent in the median state. In three states—California, Maine, and Wisconsin—the value of benefits was maintained. In all others it declined. Texas dropped 59 percent. Massachusetts 46 percent. New York City 38 percent. The subject does not end there. During this period public assistance benefits appear to have been, in effect, withdrawn from a great many persons and families. This is a murky area. Nothing can be shown, but some things inferred. The Human Resources Administration of New York City reports that from 1975 to 1982, the number of persons under age sixty-five living below the poverty level increased by half, 51.5 percent, while the number of persons receiving public assistance in New York City declined by 14.1 percent. Specifically, in 1975 there were 1,009,000 persons under age sixty-five living below the poverty level. Of these, 98.2 percent received some form of public assistance.[1] By 1982 there were 1,528,000 such persons below the poverty level, but only 55.7 percent received public assistance. Nineteen eighty-two was a year of sharp economic recession, but the drop had been steady over the period. The likely explanation is simply that as benefits remained fixed and prices rose, more and more families with any income at all found themselves above the eligibility levels for public assistance. There is no national floor for AFDC payments. A family may be well below the poverty level before becoming entitled to benefits under this provision of the Social Security Act.)

All this was making for woeful Dickensian disparities. The 1980 census would reveal that New York City had both the richest congressional district in the nation and the poorest. Of the ten poorest districts in the nation (in terms of per capita income), four were in New York City. The poorest, the second poorest, the seventh and eighth.

While this was happening, or so it appeared to me in 1980, the subject of public policy toward families had become polarized, such that there was little prospect for an end to the then-current impasse.

On one extreme a liberal administration seeking to address the subject had yielded to relatively new forces, whose principal interest was to redefine the subject. The 1980 White House conference had ended up addressing the subject of "Families." Plural. It was to be *asserted* that no one set of arrangements—parents raising children—was to have social priority over alternative life-styles, as the phrase went. In the aftermath, Gilbert Y. Steiner published his reflections on the subject with the title *The Futility of Family Policy* (1981).

At the other extreme, as I noted in 1980, "powerful forces [were] seeking to define as harmful any governmental activity that affects the family at all, and, in the name of strengthening the family, [were] advocating the repeal of programs that have succored and sustained millions of families." (Certain sensibilities are acquired in public life. The word processors at the conservative think tanks could be heard humming even then.) The Carter administration would come and go with no legislation to show for its honest-enough efforts. Honest enough; but not intelligent

16

enough. No unifying ideas appeared. I did not actually write, but certainly thought, that the ideas now were all on the other side. The impulse to reform and change had gone. And soon, I ended, would we: those of us of the 1960s who had imagined otherwise.

Five years later "the other side" has attained to a fierce orthodoxy in Washington. Paradoxically, the "neo-Malthusians"—Leon Wieseltier's term—have brought such high spirits and high energies to demolishing previous orthodoxies that the subject has somehow come alive again. Challenge is evoking response. Of a sudden the subject seems relevant once more. But if something is to come of the effort this time around, it will not be enough merely to arouse a constituency of conscience or altruism or whatever. It will be necessary to confront and to answer a formidable set of assertions that past efforts have only made matters worse and that the same ought to be expected of any conceivable future efforts. But to the narrative.

In July 1963, as assistant secretary of labor for policy planning in the Kennedy administration, apart from reading the morning papers, I didn't have all that much to do. The Labor Department had done about all the policy planning it needed for the moment. The problem was getting the policies enacted into law. President Kennedy's program was dead in the water. Unemployment had been a recurring theme of his early addresses to Congress, and he had been seeking legislation to create a general youth-employment program. As time passed, however, the economy began to recover from the recession of 1960–61, and White House concern with unemployment began to recede.

As my job was to advance the department's agenda, especially when our early prominence in the administration's scheme of things seemed to be fading, I had been looking for new arguments for a national youth-training and employment program. I had begun to suspect that the early talk of unemployment had been a kind of shorthand, a code in which the administration addressed the problem of economic growth. There was another issue. We did not know much about it, but we knew that social conditions, especially in the cities, were not as promising as the generally cheerful 1950s had led many to believe.

One morning the press carried a brief notice that General Lewis B. Hershey, director of the Selective Service System, had once again submitted his annual report to the President and Congress, and that once again roughly half the young men summoned for examination had been rejected for failing to pass the mental examination, the physical examination, or both. General Hershey's ratio was the sort of thing I had been looking for. Half the 18-year-olds in the country were not healthy enough, or quick enough, or both, to serve in the Army. Surely this argued the need for a national response. The thought of using the Selective Service System as a national screening device came instantly to mind. To link social issues to military preparedness was, well, an idea. I called Theodore C. Sorensen at the White House. He liked it.

A cabinet-level group was established, the President's Task Force on Manpower Conservation. I served as secretary. An abundance of raw data was available. For two decades, almost half the U.S. population had passed through the Selective Service System's screen; yet outside the Pentagon's journal, *Health of the Army,* almost no analysis of the data had been made. Robert S. McNamara, secretary of defense, found the figures telling. Our findings were ready on January 1, 1964, and presented to the new President by Secretary of Labor W. Willard Wirtz. The conclusions were succinct, embodied in the title, with its New Deal echo, *One-Third of a Nation: A Report on Young Men Found Unqualified for Military Service:*

> One-third of all young men in the nation turning 18 would be found unqualified if they were to be examined for induction into the armed forces. Of these, about one-half would be rejected for medical reasons. The remainder would fail through inability to qualify on the mental test. . . . A nationwide survey . . . of persons who have recently failed the mental test clearly demonstrates that a major proportion of these young men are the products of poverty. They have inherited their situation from their parents, and unless the cycle is broken, they will almost surely transmit it to their children.

From a distance, I am hesitant to assert just what it was the task force established. It could well be that the most important finding was that two-thirds of the young men of the nation *would* be found eligible for military service. But we were not functioning as social scientists. We were policy advocates in a political setting where institutional and individual interests mingled with the general high-mindedness of the time. And in the context of the civil rights crises of the time. Yet, from a distance, I would defend the judgment that the data told us something about social policies. Start with the fact that the government was interfering with a lot of people's lives; to wit, half the male population turning eighteen. There was a draft. But it was not a lottery. Some were conscripted to this elemental form of forced labor; some not. The well-to-do were not. The badly-off were not. Broadly speaking, the young men in between were. Government was treating equal individuals in decisively unequal ways. This required some curiosity as to how it had come about. And at some levels the question brought us back to yet further aspects of government. Most striking were the different rates of failure for the Armed Forces Mental Test. Unless the influence of climate or some other intervening variable is greater than generally supposed, some jurisdictions clearly were turning out brighter youngsters than others. Or if not brighter, simply more able. In some of the High Plains states, the rate of failure on the mental test was about equal to the incidence of mental retardation in a large population. In others . . . Lord help. Nor was the distribution just what a decidedly northeastern-oriented administration would have expected. The failure rate on the mental test for white males in the Fifth Army Area, roughly the Middle West and the High Plains, was 8.9 percent. The failure rate for white males in the First Army Area, New England plus New York and New Jersey, was 26.4 percent.

Lyndon B. Johnson was impressed by the report and promptly adopted one recommendation that *all* eighteen-year-old males would be tested and examined and informed of their medical or learning disabilities, if any, regardless of whether they were to be drafted. At about this time the President formally established the Task Force on Poverty, headed by Sargent Shriver. I became a member. To historians I would propose that one of the reasons the President's War on Poverty seized the day was the powerful body of information assembled by the Task Force on Manpower Conservation. One-third of the nation's youth were not fit for service.

Soon Lyndon Johnson's speeches and informal remarks included references to our report. He commenced to talk about the "peckerwood boys"—white—back in the hollows, with little education and fewer prospects. These were still years of peace in America, and such ideas were acceptable. (As late as 1966, I felt free to publish an article in the *New Republic* arguing that the armed services were excluding the black poor. They were.)

Even so, the focus of *One-Third of a Nation* blurred as the War on Poverty unfolded. Here Johnson was primarily responsible. The antipoverty program that was presented to the cabinet in February 1964 included a massive jobs program to be financed by a tax increase on, among other things, tobacco. The President dismissed this. We were, he said, *cutting* taxes that year. (Whereupon he placed a telephone call and turned away from the cabinet discussion altogether. People who thought of raising taxes in an election year!)

I fell back disappointed. The poverty program was going every which way, save the one the Labor Department had hoped for, which was job creation and a national policy of full employment, something just missed in the Employment Act of 1946. It seemed it was always like that. As noted, early in the Kennedy administration the President was forever going on about unemployment. Then the economy began to grow and the talk ceased, even though unemployment improved very little. (Again: by standards of the time. Rates of unemployment that were thought intolerable in the early 1960s are thought unattainable in the 1980s.) The government's response to poverty went off in the direction of providing services, in effect a work program for middle-class professionals.

I needed more evidence, something to make unemployment seem even more urgent. On a flight to New York, I happened to look down at a table recording the number of new AFDC cases each year since the program had begun in the 1930s. Seen as a chart, the number of new cases in postwar years rose and fell very much as unemployment rose and fell. The policy-planning staff went to work, and in a fairly short time we had come upon remarkably strong correlations between unemployment and all manner of family dysfunction. The percentage of married women separated from their husbands was then recorded each March. This was compared with the male unemployment rate of the previous month, for the years 1953–64 (the period during which both statistical series had existed). A correlation of .73 appeared. This suggested to an analyst that changes in unemployment rates might account for as much as half (i.e., the square of .73) of the changes in separation rates. At four months the correlation was .81, suggesting that as much as two-thirds of one set of changes could be accounted

for by the other. Correlations this strong are known to
social science but are not common. All the more discon-
certing then was the discovery that as we moved from the
late 1950s into the early 1960s the correlations weakened
and then quite disappeared. It was as if medical researchers
testing a new drug found it to work with great efficacy
over a period of almost fifteen years, only of a sudden to
find that it no longer worked at all.

This came to be known as "the scissors." Plotted on a
graph, the various rates would go up and down as if chained
together, but then the relation weakened, disappeared, and
reappeared as its own opposite. Without exception the indicators of social stress—separation, welfare—would now
go *up* while the economic indicator—unemployment—would
now go down. These patterns were to be found both for
whites and blacks, but most strikingly for blacks.

I thereupon moved to a large, and obviously debatable,
hypothesis. Employment, in a sense, was an easy answer
to what social problems we might have. Full employment
was then thought a feasible economic goal and was on
display in just about every nation of Western Europe. But
what if employment had lost its power to determine social
arrangements? What if deprivation, discrimination, had
gone on too long? What if disorganization now sustained
itself? Kenneth B. Clark had just then published his study
Dark Ghetto.

The dark ghetto is institutionalized pathology; it is
chronic, self-perpetuating pathology; and it is the futile
attempt by those with power to confine that pathology

so as to prevent the spread of its contagion to the "larger community."

It would follow that one would find in the ghetto such symptoms of social disorganization and disease as high rates of juvenile delinquency, venereal disease among young people, narcotic addiction, illegitimacy, homicide. . . .

Not only is the pathology of the ghetto self-perpetuating, but one kind of pathology breeds another. The child born in the ghetto is more likely to come into a world of broken homes and illegitimacy; and this family and social instability is conducive to delinquency, drug addiction, and criminal violence. Neither instability nor crime can be controlled by police vigilance or by reliance on the alleged deterring forces of legal punishment, for the individual crimes are to be understood more as symptoms of the contagious sickness of the community itself than as the result of inherent criminal or deliberate viciousness.

I now became involved with problems defined in racial terms. Not wise, perhaps, and yet race issues were at the center of policy discussions at the time and claimed attention. I now began to explore what for the Labor Department was a new set of issues, the various seeming influences of economic change on family change in the black population. I moved in that direction, encouraged by the fact that black scholars had done so long before; Clark was only the latest in a distinguished succession.

In 1950 E. Franklin Frazier of Howard University had written:

> As a result of family disorganization a large proportion of Negro children and youth have not undergone the socialization which only the family can provide. The disorganized families have failed to provide for their emotional needs and have not provided the discipline and habits which are necessary for personality development. Because the disorganized family has failed in its function as a socializing agency, it has handicapped the children in their relations to the institutions in the community. Moreover, family disorganization has been partially responsible for a large amount of juvenile delinquency and adult crime among Negroes. Since the widespread family disorganization among Negroes has resulted from the failure of the father to play the role in family life required by American society, the mitigation of this problem must await those changes in the Negro and American society which will enable the Negro father to play the role required of him.

I spoke with Clark. He seemed to agree with our reading of the employment data. In an introduction to *Dark Ghetto,* Gunnar Myrdal had stated that Clark was asking that America "recognize that large reforms, far beyond the formal enactment of civil rights, have become necessary and urgent."

This was the origin of *The Negro Family: The Case for National Action.* It was not different from hundreds of documents that are produced in Washington in most any year, save in three respects. First, in the space of weeks it became the thesis of an unprecedented Presidential address; second, when it became known, it was denounced for almost a decade; third, at the end of two decades it was at some level accepted, as if a proposition in science had bested competing hypotheses. Now it was not a "proposition in science" at all. It was the worried view of a member of the subcabinet of an American President in one of the intermittent moments of political energy and optimism when hard issues are somehow welcomed. It was a spare document: forty-eight pages, with twenty-two pages in an appendix. But it was a hurried affair. A year's work and more was behind it. The data were drawn from the standard surveys of the time. The proposition was extraordinary, but it was written for persons accustomed to extraordinary propositions. Looking back, I think that is important. It was written for an audience of a dozen, at most two dozen, men who in their brief authority had become accustomed to the uncertainties of power in Washington, which is to say that they were accustomed to making large decisions on the basis of manifestly inadequate information, concerning which there were fierce clashes of opinion even among themselves.

The report—it came to be known as a report—began, "The United States is approaching a new crisis in race relations." The paper argued that even as the nation was making triumphant progress in securing the civil rights of black Americans, dismantling a century-old system of *de facto* and *de jure* segregation of the mostly rural South, there were signs of growing social disorganization in the cities of the North and elsewhere. The best overall indicator of this was the growth of single-parent families living on welfare. If this trend were not halted and reversed, it was likely that the "civil rights revolution" would be aborted. I cited Glazer: "The demand for economic equality is now not the demand for equal opportunities for the equally qualified: it is now the demand for equality . . . of results, of outcomes." My hypothesis was that a group in which a very large proportion of children are raised in the generalized disorder of welfare dependency will have a disproportionate number of persons not equal to their opportunities. In consequence, there would not be equal results.

Absent equal results it would be judged that there never had been equal opportunity or, alternatively, that equal opportunity did not work. Either way, the historic achievements of that moment would be in jeopardy, could be lost.

I had brought three things to the study: a model, precursors, and evidence.

The model (as the article in *America* suggested) was that of rural Irish migration to the northeastern United States in the nineteenth century, a subject I had written about with Glazer (1963).

Country life and city life are profoundly different. The gradual shift of American society from a rural to an urban basis over the past century and a half has caused abundant strains, many of which are still much in evidence. When this shift occurs suddenly, drastically, in one or two generations, the effect is immensely disruptive of traditional social patterns.

It was this abrupt transition that produced the wild Irish slums of the 19th Century Northeast. Drunkenness, crime, corruption, discrimination, family disorganization, juvenile delinquency were the routine of that era. In our own time, the same sudden transition has produced the Negro slum—different from, but hardly better than its predecessors, and fundamentally the result of the same process.

The dissolution, the carelessness, the matriarchy, the predatory violence, the "protest masculinity" of lower Manhattan in the midnineteenth century, were just not that different from what was beginning to appear in upper Manhattan. So I thought.

So others could be said to have thought so as well. W. E. B. Du Bois had addressed the subject in 1908 in his book *The Negro American Family.* Nearer at hand, the brilliant and defiant Frazier had taken up several of Du Bois's themes, added his own, and published in 1939 *The Negro Family in the United States,* which forecast much that seemed now to be appearing. (Frazier, though president of the American Sociological Association in 1948, met with much disapproval.)

I had nothing specific to propose. This could have posed problems in the long run, but for the moment it was a tactical advantage. Had I gone to the White House with another jobs scheme, the reply would have been that we already had one, two, three. . . . In personal conversations

I spoke to a different level of concern that ought to be recorded, for it is at the level of nuance not easily found in archives. Lyndon Johnson's White House was a *Southern* White House. His principal aides were intensely committed to civil rights, immensely proud that they had been able to do what Kennedy had not been able to do. The civil rights acts would change *their* Texas—the Texas of racial prejudice and segregation. But to tell them, one on one, that there were other things the civil rights acts were *not* going to change (things that might be getting worse, much worse) and that this would give rise to the most searing questions of good faith—to tell them this was to win their attention.

The family report ended with the passage from Frazier cited earlier and this conclusion:

> Nothing was done in response to Frazier's argument. Matters were left to take care of themselves, and as matters will, grew worse not better. The problem is now more serious, the obstacles greater. There is, however, a profound change for the better in one respect. The President has committed the nation to an all out effort to eliminate poverty wherever it exists, among whites or Negroes, and a militant, organized, and responsible Negro movement exists to join in that effort. Such a national effort could be stated thus: The policy of the United States is to bring the Negro American to full and equal sharing in the responsibilities and rewards of citizenship. To this end, the programs of the Federal government bearing on this objective shall be designed to have the

effect, directly or indirectly, of enhancing the stability and resources of the Negro American family.

The events that followed have been recounted and need not be rehearsed, save for a few specifics. The report went to the White House on May 4. One month later, on June 4, it provided the thesis for the commencement address given at Howard University by the President. The idea to do this was that of Bill D. Moyers. The speech was written by Richard Goodwin and me in a twenty-four-hour period starting about noon on June 2. There were two drafts; first mine, then a joint product of which Goodwin was the principal author.

The President accepted the draft without change, asking (well, bellowing) only that it be shortened to his then-preferred word length. He also directed that the speech be read to the principal civil rights leaders of that time. Each in turn was quite transported by propositions that a year later each, save one, would quite reject.

Years later, in retirement, Johnson would say that the Howard University address was the greatest civil rights speech he had ever given. This is for sure: no President before him would have said this and none since has.

He went before the audience of fourteen thousand persons on hand for the graduating ceremonies and made the most advanced commitment to the cause of black equality of any President in history. Citing Churchill, he declared that the soon-to-be-enacted voting rights bill, generally deemed at the time the ultimate in civil rights achievement, was "not the end . . . not even the beginning of the end

. . . perhaps the end of the beginning." Once again blacks were being given their freedom, but, said the President:

Freedom is not enough. You do not wipe away the scars of centuries by saying: Now you are free to go where you want, do as you desire, choose the leaders you please.

You do not take a person who for years has been hobbled by chains and liberate him, bring him up to the starting line of a race and then say, "You are free to compete with all the others," and still justly believe that you have been completely fair.

Thus it is not enough just to open the gates of opportunity. All our citizens must have the ability to walk through the gates.

For many there had been great progress, the President continued (speaking in a setting that made that clear enough). "But for the great majority of Negro Americans—the poor, the unemployed, the uprooted and the dispossessed—there is a much grimmer story. They still are another nation. Despite the court order and the laws, despite the legislative victories and the speeches, for them the walls are rising and the gulf is widening." He went on to recount the facts of this widening gulf, and to insist that "Negro poverty is not white poverty"—the past had been too separate for any useful analogy. The disadvantages of the Negro had become "a seamless web. They cause each other, they result from each other. They reinforce each other."

To argue this point, the President then turned to a subject never before mentioned by an American President, never before an acknowledged issue of public concern: the condition of the Negro family, a central fact and symbol of the "one huge wrong of the American nation," a condition that had vastly improved for some but that remained anguished for many:

For this, most of all, white America must accept responsibility. It flows from centuries of oppression and persecution of the Negro man. It flows from long years of degradation and discrimination, which have attacked his dignity and assaulted his ability to provide for his family.

This, too, is not pleasant to look upon. But it must be faced by those whose serious intent is to improve the life of all Americans.

Only a minority—less than half—of all Negro children reach the age of eighteen having lived all their lives with both of their parents. At this moment a little less than two-thirds are living with both of their parents. Probably a majority of all Negro children receive federally aided public assistance sometime during their childhood.

The family is the cornerstone of our society. More than any other force it shapes the attitude, the hopes, the ambitions, and the values of the child. When the family collapses it is the children that are usually damaged. When it happens on a massive scale the community itself is crippled.

So, unless we work to strengthen the family, to create conditions under which most parents will stay together—all the rest: schools and playgrounds, public assistance and private concern, will never be enough to cut completely the circle of despair and deprivation.

The President proposed "no single easy answer." Some measures were obvious enough: jobs that enabled a man to support his family, decent housing, welfare programs better designed to hold families together, health care, compassion. "But there are other answers still to be found." To seek them out, he announced, he would convene a White House conference of scholars and experts, outstanding black leaders and government officials. Its theme would be "To Fulfill These Rights," a phrase echoing the great assertion of the Declaration of Independence and specifically intended to follow from the report of President Truman's Civil Rights Committee: *To Secure These Rights*. He dedicated his administration to this epic undertaking:

This is the next and more profound stage of the battle for civil rights. We seek not just freedom but opportunity—not just legal equity but human ability—not just equality as a right and a theory, but equality as a fact and as a result.

To move beyond opportunity to achievement. . . . To shatter forever not only the barriers of law and public practice, but the walls which bound the condition of man to the color of his skin.

His audience was not prepared for such a speech, nor yet was the press. The first accounts were routine: the President had promised equality; the ovation was "stunning"; he had received an honorary degree. But over the weekend the reporters thought again and began to assess what they had heard. Douglas Kiker recounted the reaction of an audience "accustomed to hearing national political leaders speak in traditional ways about civil rights." They had applauded the traditional lines. "Then they sat in stunned silence. And finally they applauded out of shock and self-identification."[2] No President had ever spoken so before; thereafter no serious discussion of the problem could occur without consideration of what he had said. Tom Wicker described the speech in terms of the Supreme Court decision on school desegregation. Mr. Johnson had now laid down much the same principle on a much broader scale. Separate was not equal, and in this area the races were strikingly separate. "Thus did President Johnson face squarely what must be ranked as the most difficult problem in American life."[3]

The Voting Rights Act of 1965, the second (of three) great civil rights enactments of the century, was signed by President Johnson on August 6. Five days later a riot of exceptional violence and duration broke out in the Watts section of Los Angeles. Some 7,000 to 10,000 persons took part; 34 were killed, 864 treated for injuries in various hospitals. The violence lasted from August 11 to August 17. On August 17, Moyers, as press secretary, handed a number of perplexed journalists the Department of Labor study, telling them I had written it and that it explained

much. On August 18 Rowland Evans and Robert Novak
devoted their influential column "Inside Report" to the
subject, with the simple headline "The Moynihan Report."
There now began one of the more bizarre episodes of that
singular time.

The onset of urban riots—the "long hot summers" of
that period—created an atmosphere of fear and threat and
counterthreat in which the era of good feeling could not
survive. The Howard University address was that era's
high point. But when the White House conference "To
Fulfill These Rights" met, in June 1966, the subject of
family had been specifically stricken from the agenda. Asked
why, Clifford L. Alexander, Jr., then of the White House
staff, explained: "The family is not an action topic for a
can-do conference."

In fact there was no conference. The delegates never
met in plenary session. A year of increasingly bitter rhetoric,
much of it directed at me, had persuaded the White House
that nothing good could come of the occasion.

This was a loss. Johnson's men had been seized with the
idea that something momentous could occur by way of a
national commitment to racial equality. Again, memories
fade. The family theme brought forth at first a measure
of good feeling and high expectation that strains the cre-
dulity even of someone who was there and who shared it.
When the great March for Jobs and Freedom took place
in August 1963, members of the subcabinet were specifically
instructed by the White House not to march. We could
attend, be supportive, but were not to take part in any
march on the capital. Two years later, the President of the

United States all but summoned such a march. Then it turned out that he might be summoning something he wouldn't like. It had proved a mistake to raise the subject of family. In the meantime, opposition to the war in Vietnam had become widespread and to a degree rhetorically violent. The civil rights constituency overlapped with those opposed to the war. Whatever, on sober second, third, or fourth thoughts, the White House decided it would be best that nothing come of the White House conference "To Fulfill These Rights," and nothing did. In ways, the most painful event was the gradual transformation in Lyndon B. Johnson. From being buoyantly open to ideas and enterprises, he became near contemptuous of civil rights leaders who he now believed cared only for symbols. His language was earthy and need not be recorded.

It was just as well that the White House determined that nothing should come of the conference, for by the time preparations began, the civil rights community, broadly defined, was equally determined. There was a massive failure of nerve among whites, a spare number of academics excepted. There was seemingly no untruth to which some would not subscribe if there appeared to be the least risk of disapproval from the groupthink of the moment. This was notably so among churchmen.

By early autumn a rebuttal, later published in the *Nation* and in *The Crisis* (the publication of the National Association for the Advancement of Colored People), was being circulated. The argument of the report was condemned as "a new form of subtle racism." More or less point by point, the propositions were considered and rejected as untrue or at best not proven, and that was the end of the matter. As time passed, a touch of self-congratulation appeared at "forcing" a President not to address an issue which he had by that time determined he would not under any circumstances address. (The White House conference was called for June 1966. The following January, in his State of the Union message, Johnson devoted exactly forty-five words to civil rights. To family, none.)

It should be recorded that Martin Luther King, Jr., did not like the turn the White House conference had taken, and retired, literally, to his room. He was personally gracious to me at a time when this could be done only at some risk. I was in a prison of sorts. He visited me. He spoke to the issue, first in an address at Abbott House in Westchester County, New York, in October 1965 and on several subsequent occasions, including one at the University of Chicago. The Westchester speech was as informed and understanding as anything said on the subject before or since:

> I have been asked to speak tonight on the subject of the dignity of family life. It is appropriate that a Negro discuss the subject because for no other group in American life is the matter of family life more important than to the Negro. Our very survival is bound up in it. . . .
>
> For a number of years a good many writers have tartly denigrated the role of the family. Some have asserted the family will disappear in 50 years: others have argued its preservation is hopeless because sex is now used for recreation rather than procreation. One writer

summed up the prevailing contemptuous attitude with the statement that "Family life is obviously a study in lunacy."

Some 30 years ago Malinowski refuted these pessimistic and negative appraisals with the striking statement, "The family, that is, the group consisting of mother, father and child, still remains the main educational agency of mankind. Modern psychologists agree that parenthood as the dominant influence of infancy forms the character of the individual and at the same time shapes his social attitudes and thus places its imprint upon the constitution of the whole society."

I endorse these conclusions and would emphasize one in particular. Family life not only educates in general but its quality ultimately determines the individual's capacity to love. The institution of the family is decisive in determining not only if a person has the capacity to love another individual but in the larger social sense whether he is capable of loving his fellow men collectively. The whole of society rests on this foundation for stability, understanding and social peace.

At this point in history I am particularly concerned with the Negro family. In recent years the Negro as an individual and Negroes as a community have been thrust into public attention. The dignity and personality of the Negro as an individual has been dramatized by turbulent struggles for civil rights. Conditions of Negro communities have been revealed by the turmoil engulfing northern ghettos and southern segregated communities. But the Negro family as an institution has been obscured and its special problems little comprehended.

A recent study offers the alarming conclusion that the Negro family in the urban ghettos is crumbling and disintegrating. It suggests that the progress in civil rights can be negated by the dissolving of family structure and therefore social justice and tranquility can be delayed for generations. The statistics are alarming.

As public awareness increases there will be dangers and opportunities. The opportunity will be to deal fully rather than haphazardly with the problem as a whole— to see it as a social catastrophe and meet it as other disasters are met with an adequacy of resources. The danger will be that the problems will be attributed to innate Negro weaknesses and used to justify neglect and rationalize oppression.

We must, therefore, learn something about the special origins of the Negro family. If we would understand why Negroes could embrace non-violent protest in the South and make historic progress there while at the same time most northern ghettos seethe with anger and barely restrained fury we will have to know some lessons of history. The flames of Watts have illuminated more than the western skies—they lit up the agony of the ghetto and revealed that hopeless Negroes in the grip of rage will hurt themselves to hurt others in a desperate quest for justice.

Perhaps this is an appropriate place for a comment on the structure of social problems and the degree of "fit" of political responses to them. All can agree that the "civil rights strategy" developed, roughly, in the midtwentieth century "fitted" almost perfectly with the civil rights problem addressed. In an article, "Beyond Civil Rights," which appeared in *The New Republic* in 1985, Glenn C. Loury writes:

> The civil rights approach has two essential aspects: first, the cause of a particular socioeconomic disparity is identified as racial discrimination; and second, advocates seek such remedies for the disparity as the courts and administrative agencies provide under the law.

By the mid-1960s the success of that strategy and the emergence of wholly new problems involving the individual and interpersonal behavior of a previously stigmatized and oppressed group meant that there was a poor fit between the available ideas and concepts and what might be called the work at hand. In *Beyond Entitlement, The Social Obligations of Citizenship* (1985), Lawrence M. Mead writes that my 1965 report "attained notoriety . . . for its unvarnished portrayal of family problems among blacks, but its real point was the inadequacy of civil rights as a social strategy. Government could ensure blacks fairer chances to get ahead, but it could not *give* them in any simple way the capacities to make use of these opportunities." (Mead's italics.)

I wish I could claim such prescience. I *sensed* something was different. Recall I had started out examining employment data—ours was the Department of affirmative action. Then the data went blooey, and, although I knew something had gone wrong, I did *not* know what to do. Not really.

I believe Martin Luther King, Jr. went through some of the same disorientation. I last saw him in late February 1968, not long before his death. He had asked me to speak to a meeting of the Southern Christian Leadership Conference. I expounded my by now more or less filled out view of the problems of the underclass. He did not disagree; but could only respond, "Congress is sick." He still somehow wanted a *bill*. For that matter, so did I; I suppose neither of us had yet gotten our thoughts together, and of course he would not live to do so.

He took his civil rights tactics of marches and such like north, proclaiming it a Poor People's Campaign. The last march came in Memphis, only a week before his assassination. As his very devoted but independent associate Bayard Rustin has written, the march "turned violent when some disorderly youths 'broke ranks and vandalized downtown stores.' This failure devastated him. . . ." The phrase "broke ranks" tells worlds about the disciplined elders facing the utterly undisciplined young.

By the end of the decade my own thinking had gone "beyond civil rights"—Rustin having helped mightily. I spelled this out in a memorandum for Richard M. Nixon (I was then Counsellor to the President) at the outset of 1970. Offering a "general assessment" of the condition of black America as he entered his second year in office, I wrote that there had been clear gains but also "countercurrents that pose a serious threat to the welfare of the blacks and the stability of the society, white and black." This was most evident in "the incidence of antisocial behavior among young black males. . . ." I suggested, "The time may have come when the issue of race could benefit from a period of 'benign neglect.' . . . We may need a period when Negro progress continues and racial rhetoric fades." This was a plain proposal to move "beyond civil rights," and was understood as such. However, when the memorandum became public some months later, the response was fearsome. The family report had been viewed as mistaken; the benign neglect memorandum was depicted as out-and-out racist. By mid-decade, however, various black scholars were reaching similar conclusions, notably William Julius Wilson in his 1978 study, *The Declining Significance of Race*.

In the course of the 70s, however, the civil rights strategy as applied to problems of poverty proved unavailing or worse. There was great organizational decline or demise. But by the mid-1980s black intellectuals (serving a role not unlike that of Rustin a generation earlier) had thought the matter through and were increasingly insistent that the old approach would not address the new problem. In his article in 1985, Loury continued:

There is today a great deal of serious discussion among black Americans concerning the problems confronting them. Many, if not most, people now concede that not all problems of blacks are due to discrimination, and that they cannot be remedied through civil rights strategies or racial politics. I would go even further: using civil rights strategies to address problems to which they are ill-suited thwarts more direct and effective action. Indeed, the broad application of these strategies to every case of differential achievement between blacks and whites threatens to make it impossible for blacks to achieve full equality in American society.

The midterm congressional elections of 1966, in combination with King's speech, led to two propositions. First, that the period of Great Society initiatives was over; second, that the day would come when the issue of the black family would be raised once again, but in that future, as in the all but recent past, it would be raised by blacks themselves. Frazier and King had shown, from different perspectives, not just a superior capacity to deal with the subject but a disposition to do so. In the meantime there was nothing to be done.

In February 1967 I presented these propositions in a *Commentary* article entitled "The President and the Negro: The Moment Lost." My thesis was simple. In the midterm elections of 1966 there had been a strong Republican resurgence in Congress. This was in some ways a stabilizing event. There had been much talk of the United States moving toward a "one and one-half party system," with the Democrats permanently in office and the Republicans a kind of Whig or Federalist remnant. That would have been bad for Republicans and worse for Democrats. I was prepared to welcome the two-party system back, and especially to welcome many of the new Republicans, and not least in terms of their civil rights position. Republicans in 1966 nominated twice as many black candidates for the House as had the Democrats, who put up only their six incumbents, and on the Senate side Republicans had nom-

inated and elected a black. Even so, it was clear enough
that one of those special periods in legislative history had
come to a close.

It had lasted thirty-six months in all, and just about
everyone had something to show for it. Now we would
return to more normal times, which was nothing calami-
tous. Save perhaps for black Americans. For them "the
election may turn out to have been a calamity," I noted in
Commentary. "For the second time in their history, the great
task of liberation has been left only half-accomplished."
We were reproducing the events of the Reconstruction:
"giving . . . the forms of legal equality, but withholding
the economic and political resources which are the bases
of social equality."

Now obviously I was wrong about the withholding of
political resources. The Voting Rights Act of 1965 has
proved one of the great bills of our history. But the movement "from protest to politics" would surely have a first-
order effect of directing attention *away* from the concerns
I had raised. This could be foreseen. An emergent group
does not advertise its weaknesses. But it could also be
foreseen that with time and greater confidence, the issue
of social equality would also be addressed. But for the
moment, I concluded: "The time when white men, whatever their motives, could tell Negroes what was or was not
good for them is . . . definitely and decidedly over. An era
of bad manners is almost certainly begun."

In 1972 I returned briefly to the subject in an article in
The Public Interest entitled "The Deepening Schism." (The
phrase was Andrew F. Brimmer's. More recently Martin

Kilson has described this as a "pulling-away" process.) It was something between an *apologia* and an exorcism. I had followed the data: they were moving much as expected. Glazer and I had recently set forth a general model of ethnic experience in which it was the case of "everybody up" for some newcomers, while for others it was a matter of "up and down." The Japanese experience would be an example of the former; the Irish, to keep it in the family, of the latter. In their 1967 study *The Moynihan Report and the Politics of Controversy,* Lee Rainwater and William L. Yancey had taken careful note that twice in the document I had described the black community as containing "two broad groupings—an increasingly successful middle class, and an increasingly disorganized lower class." Here, of course, was the key to much misunderstanding. I had sought to raise the issue of social class to an audience, black and white, that didn't *have* any particular problem of social class and was rather distant from those who did. In any event, the data were soon showing this schism.

The previous year, the Bureau of the Census had reported, in the flat prose it reserves for such matters, a momentous event: "There was no apparent difference in 1970 between the incomes of white and Negro husband-wife families outside the South where the head was under 35 years."

In three centuries as a society this was the first moment of income equality between black and white. True, it characterized only a limited group, but it was coming into a great legacy: the long-withheld fruits of true equality. Caste, as an impermeable barrier, was behind us. Problems of class were shown to be surmountable. This cohort had nicely surmounted them. Yet others had not, and their numbers were growing. The up-and-down process had taken hold with a vengeance. Worse, it was "being denied with a fury." I offered the view *"Poverty is now inextricably associated with family structure."* I closed the *Public Interest* article with a section headed "Envoi." I speculated on the possibility that we might commence to try to deal with the situation, but concluded that a "tentative answer would have to be that neither the will nor the capacity to do so exists in sufficient degree to make an impression on social policy." And that was that.

The 1970s were hard years for poor children. Their numbers swelled, while the resources provided them by society shrank. The combination of low economic growth and, at one point, double-digit inflation put pressures on state and local finances in much of the nation. There were limited resources for keeping up the purchasing power of welfare families, and in the main this was not done. Almost everywhere, the children were, in this sense, worse off at the end of the decade than at the beginning.

During the 1970s, female-headed families became the majority of poor families with children. By 1980 the proportion was 56 percent. In New York, where the situation is more concentrated than, say, North Dakota, the proportion was two-thirds, 66 percent. Gordon Green and Edward Welniak of the Census Bureau have estimated in *American Demographics* (1983) that overall changes in family composition in the 1970s accounted for an additional 2,017,000 poor families. The change in the composition of black families caused their real incomes, overall, to decline by 4.9 percent. Without the changes, which is to say if overall family structure had been the same at the end of the decade as it had been at the outset, the real income of minority families would have increased. Green and Welniak conclude: "These data suggest that, in the absence of changes in family composition, the average income of Black families would have increased more rapidly than the average income of White families."

In reality, during the 1970s the economic position of blacks with respect to whites worsened. A decade that had opened with the attainment of equal income between definable and significant black and white populations was now followed by quite a different "first." At least *probably*, the decade of the 1970s was the first in which as a group, black Americans, with respect to white Americans, were better off at the beginning than at the end. But this was an artifact of the greater proportion of dependent families among blacks. The more significant fact was that dependent families *as a group,* the majority being white, were worse off at the close of the 1970s than at the outset. Moreover, by this time, it was becoming clear just how large a subset in the population such families were. It was a perception that would free the subject of family from the issue of race. Or ought to.

In 1981, with the help of a range of institutions, I was able to show that half the children then being born were likely to live in a female-headed household at some point prior to their eighteenth birthday. This extended to 40 percent of majority children, 75 percent of minority. Before

47

their eighteenth birthday, one-third (32 percent) of all children then being born were likely to live in a female-headed household receiving AFDC payments.[4] In just four years the situation worsened. When Arthur Norton and Paul Glick estimated these proportions for 1984 they forecast that sixty percent of children born in 1984 can expect to live in a one-parent family before reaching age eighteen. Nine out of ten such children will be living in a female-headed household.[5] Working in parallel, as you might say, Mary Jo Bane and David Ellwood estimated that one-third (thirty-three percent) of white youth and three-quarters (seventy-three percent) of black youth then aged 17 had spent some time during their childhood in a broken family. They projected that in ten years these proportions will likely rise to 46 percent for white youth and 87 percent for black youth.[6]

In my earlier paper I had projected that one child in three born in 1980 would be on public assistance before age eighteen. That was four times the 1940 ratio. Using the same techniques, I later estimated that the 1980 ratio for New York City came out at just half. This latter must be stated at a lower level of confidence, for a city's population is subject to greater changes than that of the nation as a whole. Still, it would appear that half of the children then being born in America's largest and most important and "wealthiest" city can expect to be on public assistance before they graduate from high school.

Apart from the public schools, the AFDC program could now be considered the single most important program directly affecting the lives of children. Given especially that the new administration was then proposing significant changes in the program, none of which could be described as friendly, I had thought there would be a reaction to the paper when published. There was none.

If anyone cared, few wished it known. On March 26, 1981, the Senate Finance Committee held hearings on a proposal by the new administration in effect to repeal the Adoption Assistance and Child Welfare Act of 1980. I had managed that bill in the Senate. It was not much of a bill, but it could probably be judged the only social-welfare legislation enacted during the Carter years—notable for that reason if no other. It represented a small but significant attempt to rationalize the welfare system. And it has worked. From 1977 to 1982, the number of children in foster care declined from 502,000 to 274,000. And in 1984, some 12,000 children received federally mandated adoption assistance. If it were not for such assistance, many of these children might have remained in foster care. Under previous law, families that provided a foster home for a child orphaned, abandoned, or otherwise in need received a monthly payment. Not infrequently a bond will grow between a child and foster parents who begin to think of adoption. But that had meant losing the foster care payments, and for some such families, this was prohibitive. This was especially a loss for minority children, who comprise the greatest number of children in foster homes and who easily get "lost" in the system. A rational response was to provide a regular monthly payment to low-income parents who adopt a child who had been placed with them under the foster care program. The usual states had been doing this on their own, and the other usual states had been doing nothing. Much in the manner that the original welfare provisions of the Social Security Act simply made nationally available programs that some states had already enacted (such as "widows' pensions"), the 1980 act had made adoption assistance available to children everywhere. Now the administration proposed to "fold" the funds for this program into a block grant for social services to be given to each state, leaving the state to decide how to spend it. In principle this was good federalism, but welfare policies are an exception to this principle. Some states had adoption assistance; others hadn't and never would have had until the federal government subsidized it.

The amount of money involved was trifling, $10 million, but the issues involved were considerable: first, that children should have equal access to social services; second, that the expense of these services should be kept in bounds. (Adoption assistance payments are lower than foster care payments.) *One* national organization had asked to be heard on the subject, the Association of Junior Leagues. The Junior Leagues were founded early in this century to provide assistance in settlement houses. The association had not forgotten this origin, nor yet the primal, biblical injunction that a society must care for its children. The chairman of the Finance Committee was then Bob Dole of Kansas. Mrs. Jan Deering of Wichita, Kansas, presented the association's testimony: direct, factual, informed. Such a change would not be in the interest of children. (By a vote of eleven to eight the Finance Committee voted to go ahead anyway. The measure passed the Senate but was dropped in the Conference Committee with the House.) The Junior Leagues were heard from. Which others?

On the subject of children? Few. Even so, a new concern was making its way onto the public agenda that made it possible to discuss the issue from a different but equally valid perspective. It had begun to be noticed that the social trends of the 1970s were placing an increasing number of *women* in positions of disadvantage. The term "feminization of poverty" had appeared, and these data were as emphatic as any touching on children. In its annual report to the President for 1980 the National Advisory Council on Economic Opportunity (a creation of the 1964 poverty legislation) put the matter with some emphasis: "All other things being equal, if the proportion of the poor who are in female-headed families were to increase at the same rate as it did from 1967 to 1977, the poverty population would be composed solely of women and their children by about the year 2000."

The 1970s had been a fitful economic period for most American families; the 1980s brought the first genuine depression in a half century. From 1981 to 1983 the number of persons classified as poor increased by 3.5 million. The poverty rate in 1983, 15.2 percent, was at its highest level since 1965. In the economic expansion of the following year, 1984, the overall poverty rate dropped to 14.4 percent, but in the process the age bias of poverty became even more pronounced. Among persons age 65 and older, poverty reached the "vanishing point," as a White House announcement put it. But poverty among all children under 18 years declined to only 21.3 percent. For the first time ever the number of poor female-headed families (3,498,000) exceeded the number of poor married-couple families (3,488,000). Further, in 1984 the proportion of poor black children under age 6 *rose* to 51.1 percent.

Adding in the market value of all food, housing and medical benefits (including institutional care), the 1984 poverty rate for children under age 6 was 17.5 percent, compared to 2.6 percent for persons age 65 and over. Thus, using this poverty estimate, the rate of poverty among the very young was now nearly *seven* times as great as that for the aged.

As always, the great majority of poor persons were white, 23 million in 1984, along with 9.5 million blacks and 4.8 million persons of Spanish origin. But now, not as always, it was the case that the great majority of poor adults were women: almost two out of three in 1984. (Roughly one-third of them, the wives in poor married couples; one-third, poor female householders; and one-third, poor unrelated individuals.) More than one child in five were living below the poverty line. Of these, almost one black child in two and more than one in three Hispanic children. As Harold A. Richman of the University of Chicago testified in April 1983 before the House Select Committee on Children, Youth, and Families, "Single parenthood is now a fact of life for all classes and for all races."

It was in this setting, in May 1983, that the United States Commission on Civil Rights issued Clearinghouse Publication 78, entitled *A Growing Crisis: Disadvantaged Women and Their Children*. There was nothing new by way of information in the report; what was new was the concern of the Civil Rights Commission: "The increase in the number and proportion of women heading households was small between 1960 and 1970, but has changed markedly since then. In 1960 female-headed families were 10 percent of all families, in 1970, 10.8 percent. By 1981 female-headed families were 18.8 percent of all families with children under 18 years of age, and the number of female-headed families had increased by 2.8 million (97 percent) since 1970."

The commission report then turned to a new subject, that of "children having children." Between 1940 and 1960 illegitimate childbearing among teenagers was relatively small. But now more than half the births to teenage women were out of wedlock. "The increase in births to unmarried women has continued virtually uninterrupted for both whites and nonwhites."

The Civil Rights Commission report reflected the emergence in the early 1980s of the questions of family, and children, and of "children having children" as acceptable subjects of general public-policy discussion. This development included increased attention to these subjects by civil rights organizations and black scholars. Eleanor Holmes Norton, who had been head of the Equal Employment Opportunity Commission in the Carter administration, began insisting on family as a civil rights issue. A July 1, 1983, *New York Times* editorial quoted her: "Repair of the black family is central to any serious strategy to improve the black condition."

Earlier, the Joint Center for Political Studies, a national institution that conducts research on public issues "of special concern to black Americans," called a conference of black scholars that met in Tarrytown, New York, in 1981. Formidable talents were present: younger scholars such as Bernard Gifford of Berkeley, Mary Berry of Howard, William J. Wilson of Chicago, Norton of Georgetown; veterans such as Hylan Lewis, now emeritus professor at Brooklyn College, who had participated in planning the White House conference in 1965–66; venerables such as J. Saunders Redding of Cornell, Kenneth B. Clark, John Hope Franklin of Duke, Sir Arthur Lewis of Princeton. The conference reconvened in 1982. In 1983 it issued its conclusions, *A Policy Framework for Racial Justice.*

An introduction by Clark and Franklin set the historical perspective:

> W. E. B. Du Bois stated in the early 1940s that the most difficult stage in the struggle for racial justice in America would be reached when it became clear that fundamental inequities persisted in spite of litigation, legislation, and direct confrontation. The success or failure of the civil rights struggle, he said, would ultimately be determined by the ability of a highly trained group of black scholars to use their disciplined intelligence as effective weapons in the battle for social justice.
>
> Du Bois' prescience may be seen by the profound racial inequities that persist today. They persist despite the progress generated by the *Brown* decision of 1954, despite the civil rights laws of 1964 and 1965, despite the non-violent civil disobedience movement directed by Martin Luther King, Jr., and despite the sporadic urban riots

of the late 1960s. We are indeed at the most difficult stage in the quest for racial justice.

The report was divided into three topics, the Economy, the Black Family, and Education. The family "crisis" was discussed with all the "disciplined intelligence" Du Bois would have wished.

There was a difficulty however. There was not much analysis to be added to what scholars had established two or three or four decades earlier. This kind of enquiry had all but come to a halt in the 1970s. It was now routinely asserted that the general analysis on which President Johnson had relied had proved correct, but that was about where the subject stood.

In September 1983, the National Association for the Advancement of Colored People announced that it was undertaking a comprehensive program addressed to the problems of families that were not succeeding. Benjamin L. Hooks, executive director of the NAACP, said in a statement that "finding ways to end the precipitous slide of the black family is one of the most important items on the civil rights agenda today." He continued: "We can talk all we want about school integration; we can file suits to have more black role models in the classrooms and in administrative positions to have a cross-fertilization of ethnic cultures and background. But if the child returns home to a family devoid of the basic tenets necessary for his discipline, growth and development, the integrated school environment must fail." But as for prescriptive analysis—

what measures, what strategy, would avoid failure—there was little.

It had come to pass that after much travail a consensus formed around a particular analytic approach to an issue of social policy, and efforts began to advance an agenda that might provide an appropriate response. If I do not mistake, this followed a pattern familiar in science and perhaps now being seen in social science. Controversy is never resolved among those who begin it. Rather, a succeeding generation comes along that accepts one of the competing views, and that is that. But in this instance it was merely the weight of statistics, of events, that finally settled the case. In the interval, enquiry as such was all but proscribed. Loury (1984) writes, "It is hard to overstate the significance of this constraint on discourse among blacks."[7] Wilson and Aponte (1985) write that if the earlier analysis proved "prophetic," the result even so was that "serious scholarship on these issues was temporarily curtailed during the aftermath of the controversy. . . ."[8] Norton (1985) put it plainly that "the search for workable solutions" was delayed "for a generation. . . ."[9]

Yet—that was the least of it. Had the social activism of the 1960s somehow survived, "The Case for National Action" having been argued through, work in some coherent sense could have now begun. But it had not. To the contrary, a wholly different view of social policy had supplanted the early, admittedly often mindless, enthusiasms. Two commentaries by the all-seeing Meg Greenfield, almost precisely twenty years apart, nicely traverse the period in Washington. In February 1965, in the *Reporter*, Greenfield revealed the contents of a still-secret analysis by the National Security Council of "The Problem Problem."

Since the problem-identification boom got under way in the late 1950s, it is not surprising that many find it difficult to believe that the situation may soon be altered by a projected solution explosion—yet that is exactly what worried economists are now predicting on the basis of the mandate granted the Democrats last fall and the new amenability of Congress. The potentially disruptive effects of such a development are known to have been the subject of a top-secret National Security Council paper prepared three months ago for James Reston and recently leaked to President Johnson. Taking as its measure the Standard Problem Accelerator Indicator (number of editorials in the *Saturday Review* times new housing starts), the NSC was able to predict with a fair degree of certainty that the lag in the gap between the explosion and the boom was pointing the nation toward an unprecedented problem drain. Put another way, the NSC document constituted a stark warning that unless the emerging trend toward identification and solution is brought under control, some time before the end of the next decade there will be no more problems.

Two decades passed; things were different. The government was headed by a President whose view it was that "government is not the solution to our problem; government is the problem."[10] In February 1985, writing now in the *Washington Post,* Greenfield took note of the newly ascendant wisdom that government efforts only make matters worse.

This school of thought had now found its text in Charles Murray's *Losing Ground: American Social Policy, 1950–1980* (1984). In discussions of such issues in the capital, Greenfield reported that the mere reference to Murray's work seemed to settle the subject:

"Charles Murray" is the most fashionable of these terms at the moment. It refers to the man who wrote the book arguing that the social programs designed to improve the condition of poor blacks over the past two decades have failed and actually harmed their would-be beneficiaries. The book's thesis and its figures have been questioned, but its acceptance has been wide and its effect profound. No matter what kind of government effort you may argue for these days in this area, and no matter what obligation, be it ever so modest, you may say the government should assume, you are likely to be "Charles Murrayed," and that will be the end of the argument. The simple invocation of the book's existence will be taken as an answer to the question, even as an implied "policy choice."

Of Murray's work, more later. Suffice for now that he had set forth a comprehensive "Proposal for Public Welfare" as far-reaching as any conceived in the age of the Great Society, but reaching in quite an opposite direction:

It is within our resources to do enormous good for some people quickly. We have available to us a program that would convert a large proportion of the younger generation of hardcore unemployed into steady workers making a living wage. The same program would drastically reduce births to single teenage girls. It would reverse the trendline in the breakup of poor families. It would measurably increase the upward socioeconomic mobility of poor families. These improvements would affect some millions of persons.

All these are results that have eluded the efforts of the social programs installed since 1965, yet, from everything we know, there is no real question about whether they would occur under the program I propose. A wide variety of persuasive evidence from our own culture and around the world, from experimental data and longitudinal studies, from theory and practice, suggests that the program would achieve such results.

The proposed program, our final and most ambitious thought experiment, consists of scrapping the entire federal welfare and income-support structure for working-aged persons, including AFDC, Medicaid, Food Stamps, Unemployment Insurance, Workers' Compensation, subsidized housing, disability insurance, and the rest. It would leave the working-aged person with no recourse whatsoever except the job market, family members, friends, and public or private locally funded services. It is the Alexandrian solution: cut the knot, for there is no way to untie it.

CHAPTER TWO

"In the War on Poverty, Poverty Won."

IN January 1973, in the Alfred E. Stearns Lecture at Andover Academy, I offered what was then, I believe, a minority view that ours would soon become a more "conservative" society. My little learning was hardly up to forecasting that in 1984 some 59 percent of voters from ages eighteen to twenty-four would cast their ballot for Ronald Reagan; but it did appear to me that our politics were not at all turning radical, as many seemed to suppose.

The 1960s had been, of course, a time of extraordinary protest, and not less extraordinary pronouncements about the future. A great shift, one heard, was under way. The center, in a phrase that had gained currency at the Democratic National Convention of 1972, was no longer where the center once was. It went without saying, in 1973 that that shift had been to the left.

I thought otherwise, once again turning to demographics to see what the future might hold. James S. Coleman and I had served together on the President's Science Advisory Committee, where Coleman had headed a group searching for some generalization that might be made about the turbulence of the 1960s. The key determinant seemed to be the size of the cohort of persons aged fourteen to twenty-four. These are the people who cause "trouble" to any society; the passage from childhood to adulthood is rarely easy. If sometimes destructive, it is just as often brilliantly creative. So much for the obvious. What was not obvious until Coleman's group asked the right question was that during the 1960s the *size* of this cohort was incomparably greater than it had ever been, or would ever again be (in, say, a half-century span), and in consequence had quite overwhelmed the institutions that are supposed to look after young people and guide them into adulthood. From 1890 to 1960 the total size of this cohort grew by 12.5 million persons. Then in the 1960s it grew by 13.8 million. It would grow by 600,000 in the 1970s and decline in the 1980s.

I reasoned that when the time for locking up the dean or harassing the police passed and these no-longer-young persons turned to matters such as who would become dean or make the list for sergeant, the effect of numbers would be quite different: it would dampen spirits rather than raise them. The lecture was entitled "Peace." I proposed that the campus disorders of the preceding period would now end, but I tried to look further ahead than that. I observed that had I been asked ten years earlier who to read to find out what America was like, or was going to be like, I would unhesitatingly have said, "Read Mark Twain. Twain mostly told the truth, as Huck Finn testified, and perfectly conveyed a sense of the ebullience, the growth, the prospects, the limitless energy and potential, of our great and far, far reaching land." On the other hand, I continued, if asked then about the future, I would have recommended

Balzac. "Find out what it's like to live in a society where if you want to be a professor, you wait until the man who is professor dies. Then the fifteen of you who want the job compete. . . . One of you gets it. The rest hope for the best for their sons."

Something very like this has happened. In April 1985 *American Demographics* published an important paper by Frank Levy and Richard C. Michel entitled "Are Baby Boomers Selfish?" Their answer: Yes. The first-order demographic effect had occurred as expected. In the 1950s and 1960s the number of twenty-five-to-thirty-four-year-old workers oscillated between 14 and 17 million persons. "Since then 25-to-34-year-old workers have exploded from 17 million to over 30 million today." What could not have been foreseen was that just months after I was lecturing at Andover, the great postwar economic expansion came to an end. The economy entered a "quiet depression" in which neither real wages nor real family income grew. "In a disastrous coincidence, these baby boomers were beginning their careers just as the economy went sour." Wage growth had been the norm for a generation. Then it stopped. From 1947 to 1973 average family income rose on a steady path and never went more than three years without setting a new record. "The 1973 record still stands today." (And it continues so as of 1984.)

If we will accept that individuals tend to acquire more or less permanent political attachments in the years between age twenty-five and thirty-four, we see a great cohort of the population acquiring its political orientation during a time of real or at least relative economic distress. It appeared that it might be the first such group of young people in American history which faced the prospect that its standard of living might permanently decline. Levy and Michel note that between 1968 and 1972 the annual American Council on Education survey of the attitudes of college freshmen showed that only about half felt that "being well-off financially" was "essential" or "very important" in their lives. This number jumped in the fall of 1973 as the economy began to turn sour, and reached 69 percent by the end of the decade. Career choices were more and more frequently made with earnings in mind: law, medicine, business. Income could not be taken for granted. "It was this fear—baby boomers' perceptions that they would never live as well as their parents—that lay behind the sense of a 'vanishing middle class.' " Things could look up, of course, and probably will. But for the moment *these* family statistics will have a profound bearing on those outlined in the previous chapter. We have been a generous people, and remain such, but there is not likely to be any widespread renewed interest in the condition of the poor until the prospects of this uncertain, apprehensive middle class are settled, and for the better, and until it gets beyond the seeming selfishness of the moment.

In that sense I probably ought not to have used the term *conservative* to describe the period I anticipated. Conservative should be kept a simple word. Conservatives conserve. Sometimes, as has been written, they conserve liberalism. Indeed, a great development of democracy in the nineteenth century was the pattern that appeared in Britain, whereby a conservative government coming to office left the initiatives of the preceding liberal government pretty much intact. It made for a rhythm of innovation and consolidation; it made elections less fateful affairs, all to the enhancement of stability in a democracy. By the twentieth century this pattern was well established here. The Republican presidents of the 1920s left Wilson's program pretty much intact; Eisenhower even added to the programs of the New Deal and Fair Deal; Nixon both kept the Great Society intact and proposed some singular extensions.

This would not be so of the conservatism I anticipated at Andover. It would be a threatened, not a confident or, if you like, complacent, conservatism. The term *Reagan Revolution* had not yet appeared, but on the other hand *six years* earlier, in 1967, James Q. Wilson's "A Guide to Reagan Country," published in *Commentary*, offered the American public a prescient appreciation of the near future of American politics. Mr. Reagan had then just been elected governor of California, and something new was coming out of the West. It was in some sense "reactionary, seeking to turn back the clock to a day when life was easier, virtues less complicated, and the Ten Commandments a sufficient guide." Yet it was not, Wilson argued, in any sense a movement to return to the life of the small towns and farms that southern California electorate had left behind on the prairies from which they had migrated. It was a movement toward the values and viewpoints that the American electorate overwhelmingly endorsed in the reelection campaign of President Reagan in 1984, an electorate that felt threatened, not least by a reported explosion of social spending.

As a candidate in 1980, Mr. Reagan had quite avoided any specific commitments on social policy. But as a candidate for reelection there was the record of his first term to judge by; and to judge by the reelection returns, the American electorate was prepared to see measures proposed that, if enacted, would indeed constitute something of a revolution.

Thus, in the area of social welfare, in his second year in office President Reagan had proposed that the AFDC program be wholly turned over to the states. The federal government would assume some state medical costs in return, but the issue was one of principle rather than budget: the new administration desired to abolish a central feature of the Social Security Act of 1935. AFDC began as a "mixed" program in which each state set its own level of benefits and shared the costs with the federal government. But almost from the first, which is to say for almost a half century, the thrust of almost all discussion of the subject was to make the program fully national, with uniform payments and full federal funding. President Eisenhower, much concerned with the growth of federal power, would never have dreamed of making the Reagan proposal to turn responsibility for poor children over entirely to the states. President Nixon had indeed come forward with just the opposite idea: a federally guaranteed income for all. (And in the end, of course, Nixon did obtain a guaranteed income for the poor elderly, blind, and the permanently and totally disabled.) Not President Reagan. He wanted to undo what had been done, *because he was convinced that much that had been done had been harmful*. In a December

1983 radio broadcast he said: "There is no question that many well-intentioned Great Society–type programs contributed to family breakups, welfare dependency, and a large increase in births out of wedlock."

These had been his views, and experience in his new office did not change them, as it is said to do with many Presidents. Somewhat to the contrary, it seems to have confirmed his earlier judgments. In January 1985, three days into his second term, he told the Associated Press, "In the war on poverty, poverty won."

It would be mistaken to see this as merely ideological pessimism, reflecting, say, the biblical passage with which William H. Ayres had opened the Minority questioning on the first day of House committee hearings on the Economic Opportunity Act, back in 1964: "For ye have the poor always with you." True, the President had brought to Washington a disposition against "welfare" that had played well with audiences over many years. In Mr. Reagan's second year in office, Senator Bob Packwood of Oregon, then chairman of the Senate Republican Campaign Committee, described to the Associated Press a scene that had by then become a staple of cloakroom anecdote: "Pete Domenici, the chairman of the Senate Budget Committee, might note at a meeting that 'we've got a $120 billion deficit coming,' and the President says, 'You know a person yesterday, a young man, went into a grocery store and he had an orange in one hand and a bottle of vodka in the other, and he paid for the orange with food stamps and he took the change and paid for the vodka,' and we just shake our heads."[1] Packwood attributed the problem to what he termed

Mr. Reagan's "idealized concept of America," meaning white, male, and Protestant. Something of this may indeed have come out of the Reagan Country James Q. Wilson had described years earlier. But something had by now been added. Disposition apart, the President was now being told that the *evidence* accumulated in the course of the War on Poverty showed that it *had* failed. Here, for example, is Paul Craig Roberts, the first assistant secretary of the treasury for tax policy in the Reagan administration, testifying in January 1985 before the Senate Finance Committee:

> The growth of government has brought an enormous transformation in the nature of U.S. society. Over most of our country's history, there was neither an income tax nor a welfare system. This was a period during which the economy simultaneously absorbed millions of penniless immigrants, many of whom could not even speak the language, and rapidly reduced the poverty rate. *Today poverty has been institutionalized by the government's poverty programs, and the poverty rate no longer declines.* In the U.S. today, only the illegal poor—aliens who do not qualify for the government's transfer and welfare programs—are consistently able to work themselves out of poverty. By undermining private property rights, a welfare state restricts opportunities for all on the grounds that otherwise some will succeed more than others. (His emphasis.)

At one level this is so much blather. No one, for example, in or out of the U.S. government has the least bit of information as to whether "only the illegal poor . . . are consistently able to work themselves out of poverty." But it does reflect deeply held beliefs on the part of many who helped fashion Mr. Reagan's economic and social policies. It can be dismissed as social science; not as social theory. Recall that the "inalienable rights" claimed by the Continental Congress when it first assembled in 1774 were "life, liberty, and property." It was Jefferson's felicitous touch in the Declaration of Independence that gave us "the pursuit of Happiness" instead. But the founders of the American political system, working from Locke, clearly regarded respect for the rights of private property as a prime necessity of republican government. To hold that the income tax and the AFDC program undermine those rights is to make no small charge. This charge was routinely made during the first Reagan administration and went all but unanswered.

In combination, the prolonged "quiet depression" of the 1970s and the coming to office of persons with strong ideological aversions to government interventions as previously uncontroversial as the income tax meant that by the 1980s social legislation had not only ceased to be enacted in Washington, it had ceased to be proposed. But more was involved than the fall in real incomes, or the rise of the Cato Institute. In this period a crisis of sorts befell the policy sciences that had so flourished in the previous period. Now these are not sciences at all in any rigorous sense, but they do represent an effort to base public policy on testable propositions. As the 1970s went by, more and more policies seemed to fail their tests.

What happened?

To begin with, the claims made for the programs of the 1960s, and the expectations they aroused, also aroused a not unhealthy skepticism. Richard P. Nathan has observed that many programs were simply "undermined by anecdote." The orange, the food stamps, the bottle of vodka.

There was also a reverse of this process. A rhetoric of disparagement emerged in the 1960s. Presumably in order to maintain high levels of public concern, "spokesmen" for the poor and whomsoever would continually assert that despite apparent efforts, nothing had been achieved. (I have elsewhere recorded a conversation with an activist of the period who, seeking a new antipoverty program for her neighborhood, dismissed existing ones with the explanation that the establishment only funded programs that didn't work.) This surely contributed to a mood of skepticism.

Statistics, a kind of first-order test, were unkind. Eugene Smolensky (1985) records that "during the Johnson-Nixon years—from 1965 to 1974— . . . poverty as officially measured fell from 17.3 to 11.6 percent." But there has got to be a lead time in such movements. A reasonable argument could be made that the drop in poverty in these years came about largely as the result of events in preceding years, and in any event the decline quite halted once the Johnson-Nixon programs were in place and presumably beginning to exert their influence.

The advent of federal aid to education—after two decades of political struggle and ever-heightening expectations—came just as the scores on standardized achievement tests began a long slide. It doesn't matter that educational psychologists might object to the use of test scores as a measure of system performance; the public will accept them if the case is made. It doesn't matter that any systemwide difference the Great Society education programs might have brought about would surely have required a decade or more to appear; publics rarely think in decades. Similarly, as more federal programs were directed to the problems of dependency, the only seeming result was an increase in dependency.

But there was more. In the 1960s and into the 1970s, there was a great surge of social-science research in areas related to social policy. Much of this was ongoing work that would have taken place regardless of any political cycle. But much also arose from the times themselves. There was a good deal of what Alice M. Rivlin was to call "forensic social science," which is to say work done to develop facts that could then be used to argue a case. The negative income-tax experiments come under this heading. And then, most importantly, there was a tremendous surge of what came to be known as evaluation research. Some of this also partook of advocacy. The early studies of Head Start—not all, but most—were undertaken not only to learn how the program worked but to demonstrate that it did. Show and tell. But it is also the case that the move toward evaluation research reflected a genuine desire to introduce a measure of conceptual discipline into the formulation of social policy. At that time Washington was teeming with persons with fiercely assertive interests in particular interpretations of events.

This view was not without its politics. In the main, if one may speak from personal acquaintance, the principal social scientists involved were more than sympathetic to the general goals of the period but had professional interests also—what worked?—and a prudent concern about a lot of overpromising. Had it not been for the overpromising, the findings when they began coming in would perhaps not have been so devastating. Two asides are in order here. Overpromising is endemic to any period of political vitality and may be necessary. (The claims for Mr. Reagan's economic policies are turning out, if anything, to have been even more wildly exaggerated.) It may further be the case that existing methodologies in the social sciences have a bias toward the null hypothesis, which is to say to find little or no program effect in the short order. But neither of these propositions can be settled, and in any event the findings that came in—came in.

It fell to Peter H. Rossi, among the most sympathetic and innovative persons in his discipline, to break the news. In a review article published in 1978, he announced his "Iron Law."

"If there is any empirical law that is emerging from the past decade of widespread evaluation research activities, it is that the expected value for any measured effect of a social program is zero." More recently (1984), in the *Annual Review of Sociology*, he and James D. Wright have written:

> One of the most important lessons to be taken from all the evaluations of the golden age is that it is extremely difficult to design programs that produce noticeable effects in the desired direction. In retrospect, a reasonable summary of findings is that the expected value for the

effect of any program hovers around zero. This finding
was devastating to the social reformers who had hoped
that the Great Society programs would make appreciable
(or at least detectable) gains in bettering the lot of the
poor and redressing the ills of society.

Henry Aaron, a Brookings Institution economist who
has served in government, does not disagree. In a short
paper delivered to a 1981 conference on social experimentation he observed: "Social experiments, like most research
on social experiments, have been a force for slowing the
adoption of new social policies. . . . Social experiments, like
other analysis, show problems to be more complicated and
subtle than we had thought and that results are harder to
achieve than we had hoped."

As Aaron suggests, the 1960s and 1970s saw not merely
an increase in evaluation research but an even more significant increase in experiments seeking to discover the
effects on individual and collective behavior of different,
controlled experiences. Perhaps this overstates. As Martin
Diamond wrote on the occasion of the Bicentennial, the
United States began as a conscious experiment in government, and we have been given to experiment in the area
of government responsibilities. Recall that Tocqueville and
Beaumont came to America to have a look at the New
York State Penitentiary in Auburn. But experiments don't
always work. Auburn never worked as advertised.

From its own perspective, Aaron suggested, the new
administration ought to have been encouraging yet more
such research. But in its enthusiasm for domestic budget

cutting, it had failed to sense its opportunity. "Mr. Stockman [then the newly appointed director of the Office of Management and Budget] is making a grave mistake in trying to put us all out of work. He has not realized that we are the instrumentality for inaction. By diverting us to teaching rather than research or even to still more reputable ways of earning a living he will make easier the growth of ideas for activist social change undisturbed by critical analyses when the mood of the country shifts." Granting a measure of irony, the observation even so deserves to be taken seriously and, in my view, to be rejected.

If this is to happen, several things will be required. First of all, we need to recapture the history of the 1960s. For one thing, the Johnson administration was never nearly so carried away by the more bizarre enthusiasm of the period as it sometimes let on. Further, there is something faintly patronizing in the notion that politicians are quite traumatized by the discovery that problems are "complicated and subtle." I have lived among social scientists and also among politicians and would prefer to avoid generalizations about either; but if the issue is that of relative ease in the face of subtlety and complexity, I would be disposed to think politicians at least as well prepared as academics.

Lyndon B. Johnson was fully alive to the complexities of the domestic issues the Great Society was addressing. But in time he realized that the activists of the moment did not want to hear of such matters, and so he made a deliberate decision to conceal his own reservations. He would tell the story about the school teacher who arrived in a town in west Texas during the depression of the 1930s to be interviewed for a job that he needed in the worst way. At one point an old rancher on the school board looked up at him and asked: "Do you teach the world is round or the world is flat?" The teacher looked about for any clue as to the desired answer, found none, and replied: "I can teach it either way." When Johnson found himself surrounded by the equivalent of flat-earth enthusiasts, he thought it over maybe a nanosecond and, not without a measure of contempt, commenced to teach the world was flat.

In this specific context let me offer three propositions on the aftermath of what Rossi and Wright describe as "The Golden Age."

First, there never was a Golden Age. There never is.

On a Saturday morning early in the administration of John F. Kennedy, Harlan Cleveland found himself in a sailboat off Hyannisport with the new President and a few associates, going over some foreign-policy matters. Work done, talk turned to a new volume by Arthur M. Schlesinger, Jr., on the New Deal. The trouble with Arthur, said the new President, was that he made all those White House staff members such as Corcoran and Cohen and Rowe seem like demigods, when for sure they were no different from O'Donnell and Sorensen and Dungan of his own White House. Having known all these men, I can only agree. The President was not denigrating the talents of the New Dealers but merely commenting on the aura that distance lends to men and events.

Almost no social legislation was adopted under Kennedy. Under Johnson, we saw two magnificent civil rights acts, an enduring achievement, but which in truth did little more than enact as statute the constitutional guarantees of the post–Civil War amendments. Medicare and Medicaid were true innovations, but the rest were limited. Lyndon B. Johnson began life as a high school teacher. He wanted to be known as the Education President, but his notion of becoming so was to sign a blizzard of small bills and keep the pens on display.

The Elementary and Secondary School Act was not un-important—nearly twenty years later the federal government provides 7.5 percent of all funds for these levels of education. But the proportion has been going down of late. Apart from civil rights and Medicare, his administration had no very large legislative ideas, and he was continuously constrained by fear of being labeled a "big spender." Even with a major war in progress, his annual budget deficits (FYs 1964–69) averaged under $6 billion, and he left a surplus to his successor. It has been observed that in these years there was a division between new men with new enthusiasms—abolishing poverty, organizing communities, pursuing equality—and an older generation of New Dealers, men of the 1930s still pressing to complete a social insurance agenda formed in the early years of the twentieth century. Johnson knew the New Dealers and trusted them. He knew the general outlines of the Medicare and Medicaid proposals from the years they had been bandied about in Senate corridors and committee rooms. These were *not* poverty programs, albeit they would have a huge impact *on* poverty. They were social insurance programs available to all as a matter of entitlement. Johnson made Wilbur J.

Cohen, one of the most eminent of the remaining New Dealers, his secretary of health, education and welfare. By contrast, the Office of Economic Opportunity was awarded Sargent Shriver, John F. Kennedy's brother-in-law: not wholly a signal of presidential enthusiasm. OEO survived as a separate agency for about a decade. The Social Security Administration, by contrast, routinely, projects the income and outgo of the Medicare trust fund year by year into the mid-twenty-first century.

As for the War on Poverty, much the same. The only significant change in welfare in these years was the AFDC-UP (Unemployed Parent) program, which made two-parent families eligible for assistance when neither spouse was employed. But this came under Kennedy. As for the Office of Economic Opportunity, its budget averaged about $1.7 billion in its best years. James T. Patterson in *America's Struggle against Poverty, 1900–1980* observes of that period, "If all the OEO money had gone directly to the poor as income—and most of it did not—each poor person in America would have received about $50 to $70 per year." I argued at the time (1969) that the choice of a services rather than an income strategy just possibly, if imperceptibly, skewed the distribution of income upward.

The Great Society years are remembered as a time of great increases in the size of government and especially in the amount of social spending. This is so only to the extent that the Social Security programs of the 1930s (with Eisenhower's addition of disability benefits) began to mature and pay out large sums from the respective trust funds. But this, in a sense, was an event that had been maturing for years before the Kennedy-Johnson administrations. Much is counterintuitive in our politics. That is part of the art, I suppose. For if you would look for a *true* increase in the size of government—to 24 percent of gross national product—you must await the advent of the Reagan administration.

Second, there were not nearly so many claims made for the Great Society as now are being remembered.

In a 1984 conference on the Great Society—eras end; conferences go on—Richard Nathan, who worked for Nelson A. Rockefeller during much of this period and who, if professionally skeptical, was even so friendly to the effort, described the sometimes unreal expectations concerning social science at that time:

> Social science is *one among many* inputs to social policy. It was never otherwise. Yet there was a period of wistful expectation—a Camelot for social science—when many practitioners believed it could be more than that, a determinant in and of itself of new policy directions, or, if not that, the input with a presumed special claim and higher standing than others in the policy making process. In fact, one of the unspoken assumptions of the Great Society, which crested near the peak of the most influential period for economists in government, was that doing good in substantial measure was an intellectual undertaking, when of course it is, and has always been, a matter of desire, belief, and values.

True, but this was well enough understood. In 1966 I appeared before a subcommittee of the Senate Committee on Government Operations to propose that the Congress establish an Office of Legislative Evaluation "which would have the task of systematically evaluating the results of the social and economic programs enacted by it and paid for out of public monies." It might, I suggested, be established as a separate agency or located in the Library of Congress or the General Accounting Office. But the essential feature "must be that it will be staffed by professional social scientists who will routinely assess the results of government programs in the manner that the GAO routinely audits them." Evaluation was in that sense a development of the auditing process. (Under the leadership of Senator Abraham Ribicoff, this role was eventually assumed by the GAO. By the 1980s, some 45 percent of all GAO projects could be called evaluation research.)

I gave my testimony the title "The Crisis of Confidence" and argued simply that unless the federal government was prepared to track the results of its new programs, and be open with the public about those results, public support would fade.

"The usual whispered argument" was that to be candid about programs that don't seem to produce results is "to give a weapon to the enemies of progress." I offered the thought that the public was more realistic than generally thought and hence more accepting of difficulties, even failure. Peter Rossi had noted that "our" commitment to evaluation research was fundamentally ambivalent, one of attraction and fear, trust and distrust, both because of the possibility of negative or null findings and—more importantly—because in areas of social policy facts are simply not neutral. Social science data were necessarily political.

Most social arrangements rested on assumptions about the "facts" of a given situation. To challenge such facts was to challenge those social arrangements, an earlier observation of Louis Wirth's. It was because of this that Walter B. Miller had suggested there was a direct incompatibility between careful evaluation research and the political process.

That I was optimistic even so—pressing for the kind of analysis that in time, and in not far distant time, would prove so devastating itself—is awkwardly revealing. *So much* of all this strategizing and disputation was an affair of a circumscribed circle of fifty or so persons who happened to have been in government at the assassination of John F. Kennedy and the sudden release of political energies under his successor. They and five hundred or a thousand assorted academics and administrators and the occasional politician they happened to know or had gotten to know. When I testified to the Senate committee about "our" hopes and "our" aspirations, I was speaking of that small community. The plain fact, the large and indispensable fact, is that the attempt to address the issue of poverty in the whole of the United States came in the first instance from an informal committee of a half-dozen persons thinking up themes for President Kennedy's 1964 reelection campaign. At one point it appeared that the likeliest choice would be the emerging, challenging problems of the suburbs. Poverty held on, however, and it was, as he was reported saying at the time, LBJ's kind of program. But the electorate never asked for it; the *poor* never asked for it. Congress took it on say-so, with no structural commitment. The press was interested at first; but the press is never interested long. As for my family initiative, well, that was an affair of a dozen persons at most. All this in turn accounted for the rhetoric of the time: self-levitation.

Rhetoric *was* a problem. Hannah Arendt once observed that the "superiority" of the totalitarian elites of the 1920s and 1930s in Europe lay in the ability to immediately dissolve every statement of fact into a declaration of purpose. In the spring of 1967 I gave the Clark A. Sanford Lecture at the State University Agricultural and Technical College at Delhi, New York. The lecture series deals with local government and community life, and I described—it was no more than description—the misunderstandings that had arisen in Washington over the purposes of the Community Action programs in the antipoverty effort. There had been three distinct views—in the White House, in the Bureau of the Budget, in the Office of Economic Opportunity— and the simple fact was that the views were incompatible. Not an unheard-of event in public administration. The view inside OEO derived more or less directly from a theory of juvenile delinquency that had been in vogue during the Kennedy administration. This was the so-called opportunity theory in which deviancy was ascribed to efforts to achieve normal goals in situations where there were not enough normal opportunities to do so. Fair enough, but the essential fact was that *"government did not know what it was doing*. It had a theory. . . . Nothing more." (Emphasis in original.) A respectable theory, I insisted, but nothing approaching confident knowledge. One result was that when challenged by stronger bureaucratic competitors,

83

OEO was usually bested, to accompanying protestation. Again, not an unfamiliar event in public administration. But the lecture, when published (1969) as a small volume with the title *Maximum Feasible Misunderstanding*, was reviewed by former Kennedy and Johnson aides with a degree of animus rarely aroused by essays on public administration. Adam Walinsky, who had been Robert F. Kennedy's legislative assistant in the Senate, excoriated the book in the *New York Times*: "Basically anti-intellectual, anti-participatory, quietist, above all flattering . . . [to] political passivity. . . ."

An irony of the 1960s is that in the main the most important social science published in the period described with great clarity and equal calm the *obstacles* to social change. (To insist on difficulty is not necessarily to be daunted by it.) In the field of education, for example, the period began with the publication of Greeley and Rossi's *The Education of Catholic Americans* and was brought to a close with Coleman's *Equality of Educational Opportunity*. Each was a profoundly reserved statement, and this was more widely grasped than might be thought.

It was such research that led President Nixon, in 1970, to propose the creation of a National Institute of Education. Drawing on Coleman's work, the President's message to Congress argued that the emphasis in education had to move from inputs to outputs, which is to say results. An earlier era had assumed an easy, fairly straight-line relationship that research no longer supported; now a more complex problem had to be addressed, with final educational results being the measure of effect. The message

reflected Kenneth Boulding's contention that a major ob-
stacle to progress in education was "the absence of any
adequate theory regarding the nature and machinery of
human learning." It was further to be understood that this
learning process would require much more sustained, long-
term longitudinal work than had yet been done. We had
about exhausted the possibilities of one-time surveys. An
institution was needed that would nourish and protect work
that can take twenty and thirty years to complete.

It happens I presented the opening testimony to the
House Select Committee on Education at its February 1971
hearings on the National Institute of Education. The chairman was John Brademas of Indiana, now president of New
York University. He was for the bill (and in time saw to
its passage) but found himself besieged by arguments that
the *real* strategy of the White House in proposing "more"
educational research was to establish grounds on which to
cut aid to education. I did my best to explain that this had
become a "predictable" response.

> I would ask this Committee to understand that this
> is not a pattern of reaction confined to the field of Ed-
> ucation. To the contrary, it is almost a standard reflexive
> response to a plea for more research in the social sciences,
> or at least it has become so of late. I have elsewhere
> suggested that there has indeed been something of a
> change here. For decades, even generations, social science
> enjoyed a comfortable relationship with what were per-
> ceived as progressive social policies. In recent years, this
> relationship has become troubled. Social science has

emerged as a threatening discipline. It tells you a lot of things you thought weren't so, or wished weren't so. This is no way to win support.

Increasingly, the proposal for more research is seen almost as a hostile act.

Herman Badillo, representative from the Bronx, was troubled by this. He responded:

> I am not committed to promoting social unrest, but I can think of no greater formula for doing so than if I were to go tomorrow—as I intend to—to a group of black and Puerto Rican parents in the South Bronx and tell them that they have to show fortitude in the face of disappointment and that it may be 10 years before their children can expect to learn, because the educators really don't know what to do. I would suspect they would say that is not enough; that it is true that the educators don't know how to teach, but they haven't really tried.

I was out of government at the time and not much in a mood for this sort of thing. I answered that it would make no difference whatever whether he or his constituents or whosoever thought that what I had said was "not enough." If he wanted my advice, it would be to "go up there and tell the mothers in the Bronx that they are doing damn well with their children and they ought to be proud of them." Whereupon the questioning concluded: realities were beginning to be understood and accepted.

In sum: *There never was a Golden Age. There were not nearly so many claims made as are now being remembered.*

Finally: *There have been more successes than we seem to want to know.*

In education, to keep with that subject for a moment, inequalities associated with economic status, with race commonly a surrogate term, do respond to effort. The results are relatively weak in large systemwide programs, more pronounced in small experimental settings, but results withal. There appear to be some systemwide results. In 1982 Nancy W. Burton and Lyle V. Jones reported the findings of the National Assessment of Education Progress, which began conducting surveys in 1969: During the 1970s the discrepancy in average achievement levels between the nation's white and black youth had become smaller in five important learning areas at ages nine and thirteen. Typically, when achievement for white students declined, that for black students declined less; when whites improved, blacks improved more. The difference between the races decreased at both ages in mathematics, science, reading, writing, and social studies. In their view, "Programs designed to foster equal educational opportunity may be among the factors that have contributed to the reduction in white-black achievement differences."

In that year Stephen P. Mullin and Anita A. Summers published "Is More Better?" an examination of forty-seven studies on the overall effectiveness of compensatory education. Their conclusions were muted: "The programs have a positive, though small, effect on the achievement of disadvantaged students." The gains are greater in early years, and the "evidence is fairly strong" that these are not sustained. Even so, the reader reflects, there *were* gains.

In 1984 Launor F. Carter reported on the Sustaining

87

Effects Study of Title I of the Elementary and Secondary Education Act of 1965, the major school program of the Great Society period. A large—120,000—sample of students was followed for three successive school years. Title I, the authors of the study found, "was effective for students who were only moderately disadvantaged, but it did not improve the relative achievement of the most disadvantaged. . . ." Low-achieving students did not seem to benefit from the Title I program, and the authors suggest that "a new program with more intensive and innovative techniques of instruction should be devised for these students." Does this mark a failure of expectations? Yes and no. The 1965 legislation marked the end of a twenty-year effort to enact some form of "federal aid to education." The form that finally proved acceptable was aid to students in areas with a high incidence of poverty. True, there was a war on poverty, at the time, but this was essentially a device for spreading a limited amount of money as widely as possible through the school system. The Title I students studied by Carter received services costing about $436 per year more than those received by other students during the three successive school years beginning with 1976–77. These were modest results from a modest effort, which everything we knew then or have learned since would have predicted.

The basic data in this regard are still to be found in the *Report on the Equality of Educational Opportunity*, commissioned by Section 402 of the Civil Rights Act of 1964, of which James S. Coleman was the principal author. Robert A. Dentler (1983) judged it to make "a contribution to the study of American intergroup relations second only to

Myrdal's *American Dilemma.*" But how far less confident. Coleman and his associates found that "quality" did not much vary between schools attended predominantly by blacks and those attended predominantly by whites. More importantly, they found that where quality could be measured, the differences didn't seem to make much difference. Some—not much, nothing so much as had been assumed.

In 1972 Frederick Mosteller and I published *On Equality of Educational Opportunity*, a collection of papers from a year-long faculty seminar in Cambridge on the Coleman data. Reworked every which way, the results came out about the same. Achievement was unequal, but it was unequal at the outset. The psychologist Jerome Kagan had written that the differences in language and number competence between lower- and middle-class children are significant by the time the child is four years old, and awesome by the time he enters the first grade. Coleman could find little contrary evidence. In an introductory essay, Mosteller and I sought to restore some perspective. It had been put about that "schools don't matter." To the contrary, said we, they matter a very great deal, as anyone who had never been to school would know. It could safely be asserted that few persons think up calculus on their own. Calculus is either learned in school or not learned at all. But after a point on the expenditure curve, the influence of school as such begins to diminish, and most American schools had reached that point. (Eric A. Hanushek, in "Throwing Money at School," *Journal of Policy Analysis and Management* [1981], has shown that more-intelligent teachers produce better-educated students. This is a strong argument for raising the level of teachers' pay. But the prospects for recruiting significantly more "intelligent" teachers? We will do well to hold our own. For a century and more, half the population, the female half, was trapped in a job market in which teaching was one of the few careers available to an intelligent and educated woman. This is no longer so and never again will be.)

Intensive programs of early-childhood education clearly produce results. This is solidly recorded in the experiences of black children enrolled (before Head Start began) in the Perry Preschool program of the High Scope Educational Research Foundation in Ypsilanti, Michigan, during the period 1962–67. Most of the children were enrolled in the preschool program for two years and have been followed since, along with a control group that did not participate. In 1984 the stalwart research staff of the project reported on the effects of the program on former preschoolers now aged 19. They gave their monograph the title *Changed Lives*, and with good reason, for the program had done just that. The Perry researchers adopted a "transactional approach" that sees progress in the children's lives being determined by a continuing series of interactions between their internal performance and their external settings, a kind of domino effect in which the child brings a greater commitment to school in the first instance, is thereupon rewarded by a better response from teachers, and so on through a long sequence. An early IQ advantage over the control group—twelve points—soon disappears, which is a common finding. (Reports still to come from Ypsilanti may suggest that this is not always so.) Even so, there are changes in these children's lives. A social scientist at the National Institute of Education suggests the analogy of the booster rocket in a space-shuttle flight, which drops into the sea while the shuttle itself goes into orbit.

As for the changes, the researchers reported: "Two out of 3 individuals who attended preschool graduated from high school; the comparable rate for persons . . . who had not attended preschool [the control group] was 1 out of 2." To read the study is to gain some sense of the odds against inner-city youngsters in the age we have created. The youth are not high achievers. At age fourteen, the preschoolers were in the eighth percentile of achievement by national standards, and the controls were in the third percentile. But for every American junior high school student scoring in the ninety-seventh percentile, some other student scores in the third, and they matter too. The Perry Preschool program has shown they can be helped. The researchers could not have been more restrained in their claims:

Early childhood education is not a panacea, however; it does not solve the nation's unemployment problem. It does not solve the problem of how to deliver effective education in the elementary and high school years to the "graduates" of good early childhood programs. It does not solve the problem of inadequate housing. It does not solve the nation's crime problem. Early childhood education does give young children in need a firmer foundation on which to mature and prosper—an edge in opportunity and performance. It is part of the solution, not the whole solution.

This similarly is the message of *As the Twig Is Bent*, the 1983 compilation of the Consortium for Longitudinal Studies. In an epilogue entitled "We Never Promised You a Rose Garden, but One May Have Grown Anyhow," Lois-Ellen Datta of the National Institute of Education cites a 1979 statement by Edward F. Zigler and Elaine A. Anderson: "To the public, Head Start appeared to be a quick two-month program to make poor children smart, while to the planners, and those in the program, it was but the beginning of a long cooperative effort of teachers, health care professionals, and parents to make children physically healthy and socially competent."

And yet, on balance, the school is a weak institution compared with the home. Whatever skills, fortune, and effort it takes to provide a two-parent home make as well for better scholars. A tough-minded statement of the proposition has come from the National Association of Elementary School Principals in collaboration with the Institute for Development of Education Activities, a division of the Charles F. Kettering Foundation. In 1980 they published the study *The Most Significant Minority: One-Parent Children in the Schools*. It is the first report on a longitudinal study of the school needs of children of one-parent families. They were already prepared to state:

> One-parent children, on the whole, show lower achievement in school than their two-parent peers. . . . Among all two-parent children, 30 percent were ranked as high achievers, compared to only 1 percent of one-parent children. At the other end of the scale, the situation is

reversed. Only 2 percent of two-parent children were low achievers—while fully 40 percent of the one-parent children fell in that category.

There are more clinic visits among one-parent students. And their absence rate runs far higher than for students with two parents, with one-parent students losing about eight days more over the course of the year.

One-parent students are consistently more likely to be late, truant, and subject to disciplinary action by every criterion we examined, and at both the elementary and secondary levels . . . one-parent children are more than twice as likely as two-parent children to give up on school altogether.

And so to our paradigm. If the number of single-parent families is rising, the proportion of students least likely to succeed, least likely to respond to efforts to help them succeed, must be rising also. Hence it is argued that the programs failed and that "in the war on poverty, poverty won." As with income ratios that stubbornly refused to improve during the 1970s and in important ways deteriorated, we ask how much is this an artifact of changes in family composition? How much do averages conceal the "deepening schism," the "pulling away"? And our knowledge is skimpy. For the two decades about which we would most wish to be enlightened, the subject was all but banished from the universities and institutes where such research is done. But does this lead us to the huge judgment that "in the war on poverty, poverty won"?

It does not. To the contrary, on January 19, 1985, four days before Mr. Reagan made his remark about the war on poverty having been lost, his Council of Economic Advisors, in their annual report to the President, treated in some detail the most extraordinary achievement in the history of American social policy: the virtual disappearance of poverty among the elderly. Where thirty years ago the elderly were, in the words of the *Economic Report*, "a relatively disadvantaged group," their income levels had increased so dramatically since then that "poverty rates for the elderly were lower than poverty rates for the rest of the population."

How did this extraordinary event come to pass? The major reason—the *Economic Report* names simply one, but surely the most important one—is Social Security. The average monthly benefit for a retired couple in December 1984 was $766, which was half again the poverty line for an elderly family of two. The council's report came at the outset of the fiftieth anniversary of the Social Security Act.

Would the authors of the Social Security Act have expected these results? No, they would not have. They could anticipate the time when a matured Social Security program would put an end to penury for most of the aged and would ease the fear of old age for the rest of the population. (And in those days workers began to get old in their forties if, say, they worked in a mine—and thousands did.) But they would not have imagined that the time would come when the elderly would be in some ways better off, by certain not inconsequential measures, than the rest of the population.

Surely they would not have imagined the time would come in America when a three-year-old would be more likely to be poor than someone who had lived to three score years and ten. What they could not have foreseen is the extraordinary increase of a population of single-parent families.

By 1983 the poverty rate reached its highest level in eighteen years. The Congressional Budget Office found that the increase in child poverty after 1979 was most likely to be related to "the severe back-to-back recessions of 1980 and 1981–82, the rapid inflation of 1979–80, and reductions in income-maintenance programs."[2] But over the two decades the principal correlate had been the change in family structure, the rise of the female-headed household.

The term *feminization of poverty* is useful. It gets halfway to the point, but only halfway. It is not females who suddenly succumbed to poverty during this period but children, of whom slightly more than half are male. The *age bias* of poverty is now its most pronounced feature. Consider this perversely inverted triangle of the 1984 poverty rates.

- 24.0 percent among preschool children;
- 20.3 percent among school-aged children;
- 12.4 percent among the elderly; and
- 11.7 percent among non-elderly adults.[3]

As noted earlier, the poverty rate for the elderly—12.4 percent in 1984—drops to 2.6 percent after taking into account in-kind income. Nothing like that decline occurs for persons under sixty-five. In the one case the decline is three-quarters; in the other only one-quarter. Applying that percentage to preschool children, their poverty rate was 17.5 percent. This is to say that the rate of poverty among the very young in the United States has become nearly seven times as great as among the old.[4] In 1984 there were 33,700,000 Americans living below the poverty line. Of these, 16,440,000 lived in female-headed families. Of those over 16 million persons, 6,772,000—42 percent—were children. In round numbers, in 1984 half the poor in America (47.8 percent) lived in female-headed families.[5] If the trend line of the past two decades has continued, as there is every reason to suppose, the 50 percent mark will by now have been reached. Poverty will have been statistically transformed.

Over half the 13.3 million poor children in America (62.9 percent) are white. Another third (33.1 percent) are black. One-sixth (17.7 percent) are of Spanish origin.[6]

It is reasonable to assume that historically the proportion of poor children has been pretty much the same as the proportion of poor adults. Using 1983 data, we see this in the "nonminority" group. Among the nonelderly adult population, nonminority persons make up 59 percent of the poor in their age groups, but nonminority children account for only 49 percent of the poor children. In cohort terms, their children are somewhat better-off already and presumably are going to stay better-off. This may be a statement beyond the strict evidence, but it is not an absurd statement. On the other hand, adult blacks make up a quarter (26.2 percent) of the poor in their age group, while black children make up nearly one-third (31.3 percent). Black children are more likely to be poor than are black adults. This is not progress. Elderly blacks make up only a fifth (21.3 percent) of the poor in their age group.[7] Using the reduction ratios that take in-kind income into account, we can state that black children are four times more likely to be poor than are elderly blacks.

The family effect is now pervasive. In their recent paper "Poverty and Family Structure: The Widening Gap between Evidence and Public Policy Issues," William Julius Wilson and Katherine M. Neckerman of the University of Chicago cite estimates that "the turn of the century will see 70 percent of all black families headed by single women. . . ." Such households are concentrated in central cities, where in 1983 the poverty rate for all school-age children was 30 percent.

But poverty has returned to cities generally.

In 1959, 27 percent of the nation's poor were concentrated in central cities. By 1983, 36.5 percent of Americans living in poverty lived in central cities—a one-third increase over these years. The poverty rate of cities was higher in 1983 than in 1959.

Emanuel Tobier of New York University calculates that in 1984 "more than 40 percent" of New York City's children were poor. The city's poor population, he observed, "is increasingly dominated by women and children."[8] In a 1985 study done for the Chicago Urban League, Pierre deVise reported that "nowhere in the nation, and nowhere in the world where birth statistics are kept, is the evidence of rapid family disintegration more glaring than in Chicago's ghettos." DeVise found that 66 percent of the city's black children lived in female-headed households, up from one-third in 1970.

The social structure of public housing in large cities has declined much in the manner Rainwater first detected in the 1960s. A 1984 survey by the Citizens Housing and Planning Association found that 54 percent of the units in housing authorities managing 1,250 or more units were occupied by female-headed households. Leaving out New York City, the proportion becomes 69 percent.

It needs so very much to be emphasized that, as such, youths from female-headed households are not necessarily more likely to have difficulties than other children. It seems to be more a matter of these children being more likely to find themselves in secondary situations that do make for different probabilities. Children from female-headed households are not as such more likely to have trouble with the law. But the home life of such children is more likely to have features that make for criminality. In his review of *Crime and Human Nature* (1985) by James Q. Wilson and Richard J. Herrnstein, John Kaplan writes:

> It appears that if, in the first three and a half years, a child lacks what psychologists call "a secure adult attachment to a primary caretaker," that child will grow up simply not caring for anyone's approval and lacking any sense of guilt. . . . The illegitimate birth rate in the United States—like our crime rate—is far greater than that of any other Western nation. Though our data are

not very good, it does make sense to believe that these unprepared mothers are the ones most likely to be overwhelmed by the difficulties of bringing up the children who, 10 years later, are the ones most likely to begin careers in crime.

Freeman and Holzer (1985) report that about one-fourth of all income of inner-city black youths is from crime. Similarly they find that while youths from female-headed households do not do particularly worse in finding jobs than youths from other families, "certain characteristics of families matter greatly." Put plain: "persons whose families are involved with major public programs for disadvantaged families do worse in the job market." Youths from welfare homes do far worse than those from nonwelfare families with the same incomes and characteristics. Youths living in public housing do less well. No one has been able to tease out the direction of causality, save that it clearly is not a matter of economic man making rational calculations. Freeman and Holzer conclude, "Since the 'loss' of welfare benefits is slight when youths work, the problems of youth in welfare households cannot be explained as simply a 'rational' response to economic incentives. Instead they are more likely related to other factors such as information and 'connections' or attitudes and 'work ethic.' " Will the reader think back to the time when he or she first acquired a fixed attachment to the work force and recall the amount of help received from others. What if there are no others?

There is a sense in which these circumstances crept up on us. A flurry of comment two decades ago subsided; the trends did not. It is perhaps not surprising, then, that demographers first broke the silence and commenced what could be termed a structural analysis of the changed incidence of poverty among groups of different age and family formation.

In 1981, Kingsley Davis and Pietronella van den Oever, contended in *Population and Development Review* that something resembling "class struggle" had broken out between age groups in the United States:

> Our view is that in the past, family solidarity was the force that minimized the struggle between the generations and provided a division of labor by complementarity. In contemporary industrial societies, however, changes in the family and a simultaneous aging of the population have shifted the context of intergenerational relations to the wider economy. This has led to a nascent conflict of interest, a sort of "class struggle," between old and young.

In 1984, Samuel H. Preston of the University of Pennsylvania gave the Presidential Address of the Population Association of America, the title, "Children and the Elderly: Divergent Paths for America's Dependents." Preston began by examining the seemingly logical hypothesis that great growth in the elderly population in the 1970s—"a higher rate than [that of] the total population of India"— would leave the elderly rather the worse off compared with other age groups, especially children, the other dependent age group. But no. The opposite happened, as the Council of Economic Advisors was soon to confirm.

Preston then turned political scientist. Much of this transformation could be shown to involve actions by government. Whose influence on government was greater? Clearly, the elderly and age groups coming along who see themselves as soon to be elderly. Children can't vote; and childhood is behind the rest of us. Preston comments: "Children's only remaining source of political influence is parents acting on behalf of their progeny." And where are these parents? More and more, one is missing. Sixty-five percent of the increase in the number of children living in poverty between 1970 and 1983 occurred in households headed by a woman. Only 38 percent of voters live with a child, he continued. Hence the new politics of redistribution. More and more resources go to the elderly. Because these resources come from the working-age populations that must also care for children, they are, indirectly, a transfer *away* from children. Simultaneously, transfer payments *to* children are reduced or allowed to lag. He calculated that federal expenditures on children are about a sixth of the total spending on the elderly.

Whereupon Preston asked: "Do we care?" This need not be a cry of indignation. The question can be stated in quite neutral terms: *Do* we care? A certain plausibility attends the proposition that the future is likely to be considerably affected by how we answer. I believe we ought to care. But given the equivocal nature of much research, the absence of any direct political stirring, and the absence of any easily available resources, the question Do we care? will be *answered* in the first instance by our ability to state with some concision just what it is we would do if we did. And so we return to the question of family policy.

CHAPTER THREE

Common Ground?

I N the opening passages of his 1985 State of the Union Address, President Reagan spoke of the achievements of his first term and the promise of his second. The American people, he said, had brought forth "a nation renewed—stronger, freer, and more secure. . . . New freedom in our lives has planted rich seeds for future success." First of all: "For an America of wisdom that honors the family, knowing that as the family goes, so goes our civilization . . ." At the close of his address he turned to the balcony of the House of Representatives and introduced "an American hero," Mrs. Clara Hale, seated there next to the First Lady, which is to say the honored guest of that state occasion.

The President spoke: "She lives in the inner city where she cares for infants born of mothers who are heroin addicts. The children born in withdrawal are sometimes even dropped on her doorstep. She helps them with love."

The manifest sincerity of the President's belief that "as the family goes, so goes our civilization" seemed, even so, incomplete. Much of his political career had centered on the celebration of family and "traditional values." (Wilson in his 1967 article had focused on that single-family house, however modest, the center and symbol of all in Reagan Country.) None could doubt the President's conviction. Yet clearly it did not occur to him, nor to his speech writers (Mrs. Hale's really quite splendid story had been told in the September 1984 issue of *Reader's Digest*), that her work was not wholly reassuring to anyone concerned with the well-being of the American family.

"Go to her home some night," Mr. Reagan said, "and you'll see her silhouette against the window as she walks the floor, talking softly, soothing a child in her arms." There is a problem of detail here. Hale House, at 154 West 122d Street, is a five-story tenement. Only with some difficulty will the passerby see through even first-story windows in this burnt-out section of the city. Not exactly candlelight gleaming through the sycamores on the banks of the Wabash far away. Nor yet a split-level ranch in Orange County.

Nor did the President seem aware that to the degree that he was honoring the work of Hale House, begun in 1969, as well as the character of its founder, he was honoring a government program. In the New York Fiscal Year 1983–84, Hale House received $297,573 from all sources, of which $272,299 came from the federal, New York State, and New York City governments. Far the largest amount came from the foster care, child welfare services, and adoption assistance programs of the federal government, for which state and local governments provide matching grants.

The subject of foster care funds was touched on earlier. At the time the Reagan administration took office, under the Social Security Act as amended, a child placed in foster care was entitled to foster care assistance. This is to say the foster parents would automatically receive child support payments, and these without limit to number. Foster care was seen as merely an aspect of the AFDC (Aid to Families with Dependent Children) program, save that in these cases the child had no parent or parents. One of the administration's first proposals, however, was to consolidate a variety of child welfare services into a block grant, to be given to states to spend as they chose for general purposes, and with an overall funding cut of more than 25 percent. (The measure also proposed to abolish adoption assistance, a subject that was briefly discussed earlier.) The essential fact of the new arrangement was that foster care would no longer be an entitlement. The measure passed the Senate, but foster care was preserved by the House. The next year the administration tried again, and again failed. Thereupon it set out to "cap" the amount of funds that the Administration for Children, Youth, and Families—where the program is administered—could spend, which in effect limits the entitlement. And so the dispute continued.

Nor yet, we may suppose, had anyone told the President that less than a block from Hale House, on Seventh Avenue between 122d and 124th streets, at just about the time lights go on, enabling Mrs. Hale's reassuring silhouette to be observed, a drug exchange opens. Three to four to five hundred men stand about on the sidewalks—much as in the Curb Exchange of nineteenth-century commerce in downtown Manhattan (this is uptown)—and trade narcotics. Here and there a federal agent will be found purchasing drugs to keep up-to-date the government price index for heroin, cocaine, and other assorted substances. No arrests are made. Thus we are at the end point of a sequence of federal crimes—illegal smuggling, illegal possession, illegal sale—that the federal government has quite failed to prevent, much less to punish, with grim consequences for portions of the American population who might otherwise think of themselves as being protected by their government.

A conservative slogan of sorts gained currency in these years. The task of the federal government, it held, was to "deliver the mail and defend the coast." The mail hasn't been getting through to Harlem very well these days, so many of the apartment mailboxes having been jimmied to steal welfare checks with which to purchase drugs that had made their way uptown, in consequence of the manifest failure of government to defend the coast. The President, like his predecessors, had taken an oath to "faithfully execute the office of President of the United States," which office includes the responsibility to enforce the laws of the United States. But to the contrary, the narcotics laws were not being enforced. Mr. Reagan was in a position to celebrate Mrs. Hale as an American hero because the federal government had not seen to the enforcement of its laws, and consequently the environs of Hale House teemed with drug addicts. Is this not curious?

(At moments this dissociation attains to the comic. The following February, as Mr. Reagan's attorney general prepared to leave office, a booklet was prepared reviewing his accomplishments. Among these was the merger of the Drug Enforcement Administration into the Federal Bureau of

Investigation. The thirty-three-page booklet, *Challenge, Change and Achievement: The Department of Justice 1981– 85,* quotes the departing attorney general:

> Prior to 1982 the number one federal law enforcement agency—the FBI—was not being used against the nation's number one law enforcement problem—narcotics trafficking. For the first time the FBI was enlisted in the anti-narcotics battle. . . . At the same time, the Drug Enforcement Administration was formally merged with the FBI, producing a truly unified federal investigation effort.

A photograph showed the merger ceremony. In point of fact nothing of the kind had happened. The two agencies had merely agreed to cooperate.)

Somehow these connections are not made. As for anything government might do or be responsible for, the President simply said that four years earlier "we began to change . . . our assumptions about government and its place in our lives." Which was to say less government. "Out of that change has come great and robust growth—in our confidence, our economy, and our role in the world." Now, of course, nothing of this sort had happened. The federal government was by now consuming the largest proportion of gross national product of any peacetime year in history. But it ought not be expected that political rhetoric will be open on such matters. Would it have been too much, however, to ask that somewhere in an address that began with a strong statement about family—asserting that family well-being was something "America" knows about—there be some acknowledgment that not every trend was reassuring?

The 1983 income statistics were available at this time. They were surely grounds for congratulations. Median family income in 1983 increased 1.6 percent after adjusting for low inflation. This was the first statistically significant increase in family income since 1978. Note, however, real median family income had still not passed the $27,017 peak of 1973. The 1983 level was $24,580. Median family income levels in the 1981–83 period were at their lowest level since 1968. Note further that female-headed households showed no significant change, remaining at $11,790. The 1983 poverty rate was 15.2 percent, the highest since 1965. In that year the number of persons classified as poor increased by 868,000, bringing the two-year cumulative increase (between 1981 and 1983) in the number of poor to 3.4 million.

In the past, the number of poor had generally decreased when average family income increased. This did not happen in these years, owing partly to a huge increase in the number of female-headed families and of unrelated (largely single) individuals. Their incomes did not rise. Certainly, economic factors—particularly the lingering effects of the 1981–82 recession—contributed to this. Nevertheless, *for the first time since the federal government began keeping track, there was a simultaneous increase in wealth and poverty within the population.* Now this is something we heard a lot about in the last century. Half of mankind, or thereabouts, is committed to a doctrine that insists this is the way capitalist society will go. It isn't. There is no "immiserization" of

the proletariat to be seen in these statistics. There is, however, a continuing change in family structure ineluctably
associated with poverty.

The story does not change in the most recent statistics,
for 1984:

- About 7.3 million families were below the poverty line;
  3.5 million were married-couple families; 3.8 million
  were single-parent families, of which 3.5 million were
  families headed by a female householder.
- The majority of poor persons, 23.0 million, were white;
  9.5 million were black; 4.8 million persons were of Spanish origin. (Persons of Spanish origin may be of any race
  according to the Census Bureau.)
- In 1984, 61 percent of poor adults were women; more
  than three-fourths of all the poor were either adult women
  or children (under age eighteen).
- More than one youth in five (21.3 percent) were living
  below the poverty line in 1984—of these, almost one
  black child in two (46.5 percent) and more than one in
  three (39.0 percent) children of Spanish origin. The poverty rate for children in female-headed households was
  much higher (54.0 percent) than that for children in all
  other families (12.5 percent).
- When the market value of food stamps, school lunches,
  subsidized housing, and payments for medical benefits
  are added to cash income, poverty rates decline, but in
  quite different magnitudes for different age groups. The
  poverty rate for children under 18 drops to 14.9 percent;
  that for the elderly, to 2.6 percent.

- For children under six, the poverty rate is nearly seven times that of the elderly: 17.5 percent compared with 2.6 percent.
- In 1984 approximately 33.7 million persons were poor. Children, who represented less than 27 percent of the overall population, comprised 40 percent of the poor. Children were the only age group overrepresented in the poverty population.

It is fair to assume that the United States has become the first society in history in which a person is more likely to be poor if young rather than old. Nor is ours some Nordic enclave in which only a handful of persons could be said to be poor, such that proportions do not signify anything special. There are a large number of poor persons in the United States, and they are disproportionately young. Children displaced the elderly as the poorest age group in 1974. In 1959, the child poverty rate was 26.9 percent, one-fourth less than the elderly poverty rate of 35.2 percent. By 1984, the child poverty rate was 21.3 percent, nearly three-fourths greater than the elderly poverty rate of 12.4 percent. Over the period, poverty rates for the elderly steadily declined, while for children poverty rates stayed in the range of 15 percent. Commencing in 1979, however, while the poverty rate among the elderly continued to decline, that of children rose sharply and is now approaching one-quarter.

Wide disparities in the main benefit programs serving children and the elderly contributed to this dramatic change in the composition of poverty.

- Between 1970 and 1984, the average expenditure per Social Security OASI (Old-Age and Survivors Insurance) recipient increased 54 percent in constant-dollar terms while the average AFDC expenditure per recipient declined by 34 percent.
- Social Security benefit levels were deliberately increased in the early 1970s to bring down the elevated poverty rates that prevailed among older persons at that time; in 1971, the year before a 20 percent ad hoc benefit increase was granted in Social Security, the elderly poverty rate was 21.6 percent. (The poverty rate among children, 21.3 percent, is now similarly elevated.)
- In 1983, Social Security OASDI (Old-Age, Survivors, and Disability Insurance) payments to children and their parents (in the main, survivors insurance received by dependents of deceased workers) exceeded federal expenditures for AFDC benefits in that year. In 1983, the OASDI program paid an estimated $10.5 billion to 3.1 million children and to 700,000 parents caring for children. These OASDI benefits exceeded federal expenditures for AFDC benefits in that year by $3 billion (or 40 percent).

In the language of the parliamentarian, the question recurs on the motion to proceed. Twenty years ago in the *America* article, I proposed that the "formulation of a national policy concerning the quality and stability of family life could be the cornerstone for a new era of U.S. social legislation. . . ." The essence of family policy is that it focuses on the outcomes of *other* policies. Apart from employment, of which more later, the national, state, and local governments carry on various social programs that are assumed to bring about desirable social results. But in and of themselves these results are partial and inconclusive. Family welfare tends to be a summation of such results. In particular, assuming some general categories of well-being can be agreed on, it alerts us to trends that can be counterintuitive and otherwise hidden from view. Thus in 1965 we could note that the economy was flourishing and unemployment at the lowest levels in memory, yet could see from *family* data that we were heading for the present troubles if existing trends continued.

That was in a previous political era. What of the present? Surprisingly perhaps, or perhaps not, there appears a strikingly parallel evolution. About three and one-half years into the Kennedy-Johnson administration, the Policy Planning staff of the Department of Labor, relying heavily on census data, began to investigate trends in family structure, and the findings were thereafter passed to the White House. Three and one-half years into the Reagan administration, the cabinet was presented with the findings of a White House task force, directed by a former head of the Census Bureau, Bruce Chapman, on exactly the same subject.

The task force report was entitled "Why Not 'Fairness' for Families?" Its thesis was straightforward: "The poverty issue . . . would disappear almost entirely with the improved economy except that the rates of divorce and formation of single-parent households remain high." This development is then explained in terms of the thesis of *Losing Ground* but goes on to impressively large and specific policy recommendations. (Of which more later.)

Business-oriented conservatives began also to address the subject. The National Forum Foundation, a "non-partisan tax-exempt research and education foundation," one of the many conservative think tanks that flourish in Washington in the 1980s, with Senator Jeremiah A. Denton of Alabama as its chairman and Joseph Coors on its board of directors, devotes itself to three subjects: "National Security, Family, Welfare Reform." The group clearly approaches family issues from a governmental perspective, regarding the subject as essential in developing and advancing a conservative political agenda. The Forum's publication for January 1985 reported, "It is becoming infinitely clear that the nation is experiencing an alarming rate of family disintegration."

There was in fact at this time a growing sense within conservative intellectual circles that it was no longer sufficient simply to oppose liberal welfare policies. There was a need, as one essayist put it, for "an alternative, a conservative vision of the welfare state in America."[1] Much attention is paid to the "mediating-structures approach," a concept of writers as various as Robert Nisbet and Peter and Brigette Berger, which argues the need for modern societies to buffer encounters between the state and the individual. If Alva Myrdal wrote from the left, these writers generally address matters from the right; and yet they find themselves dealing with family, church, local associations. (Although church does not loom large with Myrdal.)

The younger conservative writers, having in a sense "missed the war" and its awful simplicities, found themselves in a conservative Washington where it was obvious the state was not going to wither away, and began to ask how the state might advance a conservative vision of society.

A young political scientist, Peter Skerry (1983), rediscovered Head Start, or rather, observing that it had survived even in the early Reagan budget, he asked why and discovered that the Head Start program that had actually evolved was not at all what liberals had planned but, rather, many things that conservatives might very well have hoped for. Head Start was disorganized, decentralized, unintegrated. Excellent. As an educational process it had the supreme advantage of not being compulsory. First rate. As an institution—a network of more or less autonomous institutions—it had the supreme advantage of being in constant jeopardy. Even better. In consequence morale was high, and a great deal of work was done by volunteers. The kids might or might not have been learning anything much, but there was no stigma of welfare about Head Start centers, and even though the state had created them, they were something more than a creation of the state. *Quod erat demonstrandum.*

Skerry saw in these neighborhood groups something of the qualities of the old political clubhouses, which reformers had destroyed without knowing what would be missed. "Unfortunately," Skerry wrote in *The Public Interest* (Fall 1983), "all this seems utterly lost on conservatives. With tuition tax credits they seek to recapture the virtues of the neighborhood school, yet they remain oblivious to the fact that a program such as Head Start never lost those virtues."

To say yet again, what emerges here is the realization that in the nature of modern industrial society, no government, however firm might be its wish otherwise, can avoid having policies that profoundly influence family relationships. This is not to be avoided. The only option is whether these will be purposeful, intended policies or whether they will be residual, derivative, in a sense concealed ones.

This sensibility does not come readily to American government; and yet it may be rising. Social historians study the diffusion of social issues and responses; there is much trans-Atlantic movement, in the main westward, at least until of late. Consider again President Reagan's State of the Union Address and Mrs. Hale. The family connection was there, in full view of the President and his advisors, yet it was not quite taken in.

In 1969 I became assistant for urban affairs, later counselor, to the President. I brought two priorities to the assignment: first, welfare reform; second, I wished to see the drug traffic placed on the agenda of American foreign policy.

(On the President's agenda, that is. Peter Reuter has pointed out that from the time of the Shanghai Treaty of 1909, the United States has been looking to foreign nations to curtail the drug traffic. Our own efforts have been minimal. In the early 1960s the Federal Bureau of Narcotics, as it then was, had fewer than 450 employees and only 5 agents posted in Europe. In the manner of the Federal Bureau of Investigation of that era, a much publicized agency head maintained a personal and institutional reputation for toughness by avoiding the toughest problems.)

In August of that year President Nixon proposed the Family Assistance Plan, a guaranteed income that would replace welfare assistance. Directly thereafter I flew west from San Clemente to India, then Turkey, then France, meeting with officials there, telling of the United States President's concern about the flood of heroin then coming into the United States. (Not then from India, where huge amounts of opium are grown but under effective government supervision that was well worth a look.) The drug traffic of that time consisted largely of opium grown in Turkey, processed into heroin in southern France, and thence smuggled to New York. Heroin-related deaths had passed the thousand-a-year point in New York City alone.

I was courteously received in Istanbul by the Turkish foreign minister, Ihsan Sabri Laglayangil. He knew well enough that poppy was grown in Anatolia; poppy seed is part of the Turkish national diet. But he knew nothing of drug use, and if the United States wanted Turkish farmers to farm differently, we would have to pay them to do so. Which was reasonable, and which, in time, we did. But in Paris the matter assumed quite different levels of seriousness. Heroin use had appeared in France. Among youth! There had been deaths. As I made my way to and from Paris that autumn, the concern there grew. The Cultural, Family, and Social Affairs Committee of the French National Assembly began hearings. On October 17 *Le Monde* reported that in a session the previous day, a government official had stated that the number of persons in France questioned by the police about drugs had risen from 107 in 1965 to 255 in 1969. The article carried the headline "Eight Out of Ten Minors Who Are Drug Addicts Come from Broken Homes." On October 24, there was a general debate on the subject in the National Assembly. One Deputy ascribed youth drug addiction to a crisis in Western civilization and insisted that the government must respond. A vast written and oral campaign on film and television was required. Others agreed and added thoughts of their own. French youth faced decimation if government did not act.

Note there was manifestly a crisis of drug abuse in the United States. (Crime associated with heroin use became epidemic in Washington, D.C., that year. A group of eminent citizens of the capital had asked to meet with me, as the assistant for urban affairs. Their proposal was direct. They wished the President to order the regular army into the capital to restore and maintain order.) But government in the United States was doing nothing, or as near to nothing as makes no matter, to limit the availability of drugs. On the last of these visits to Paris, in December, a kind of summit occurred at a lunch given by our ambassador, Sargent Shriver. On the American side were Egil Krogh, Jr., of the White House staff, who had taken on the task of getting a serious program started; John E. Ingersoll, director of the Bureau of Narcotics and Dangerous Drugs; and Anthony S. Pohl of the New York City Police Department. The French side was headed by Jean Dours, *directeur général de la Sûreté.* Now the name of the *directeur général de la Sûreté* is known in France, but he does not give interviews and rarely meets with foreigners. This was different: an American President was concerned about an issue that involved French youth as well. I spoke for our side, citing in particular the number of deaths in Manhattan, it being the worst case and the one most easily grasped by a Parisian. At the end the French saw that they had to

do something. (And in time they did.) But their bewilder-
ment was scarcely concealed. The Americans were just *now*
coming to tell us about a plague ravaging their cities, their
youth? Lunch finished—vichyssoise, poularde louisianne,
cauliflower hollandaise, salad, cheese, pears, coffee—our
guests rose. In the hallway I helped the head of the *Sûreté*
with his coat. He did not thank me. He turned, rather,
looked straight at me, and asked in a tone of incredulity
tinged with disdain: "What kind of people are you?"

Well, for starters, we are not Frenchmen. Our ethnic
and religious diversity has made for a rather strong sense
of sharing within groups and for uneasiness when this norm
is extended to the nation as a whole. There is not an
American nation in the sense there is a French nation.
There is an American state; but even that is different. We
know more of covenant than of sovereignty. We like to
see ourselves as individualists. "Root, hog, or die," the
Southerners will say. "Some have plenty—some have
none, / That's just the way with the Kansas Run," goes
the frontier ditty. Yet we are a surpassingly generous people, not least one supposes because we are, in the end, so
blessed, so well-off generally. This makes for anomaly. We
have a reasonably comprehensive, generous welfare state
but either don't know this or deny it. (Recall President
Kennedy's plaint.)

In the first quarter of 1984, half (47 percent) of the 83.6
million nonfarm households in the United States received
benefits from one or more government programs. Some
30.6 million received nonmeans-tested benefits, including
more than 23 million who received Social Security or rail-

road retirement. Another 2.7 million received unemployment compensation. Some 16 million households received benefits from one or more means-tested programs. AFDC or other cash assistance went to 3.9 million households; Supplemental Security Income to 2.9; food stamps went to 6.5 million households; free or reduced-price school meals to 5.9; Medicaid helped 7.6 million households (nearly one-tenth of the population); while 3.6 million benefited from public or subsidized rental housing.

To say again, every other American household had one or more members participating in one or more government social-welfare or social-insurance programs. Yet in the main the American public will not acknowledge that the insurance aspects of Social Security exist (survivors benefits, for example), and assert with great conviction that retirement benefits will not be available when their turns come. (A *Washington Post*–ABC poll in 1985 found that 55 percent of persons aged 31–44 were of this view.) In general, as persons get nearer to retirement age, they become more persuaded that they will receive retirement benefits, but with great wariness; later, they are readily enough persuaded that the benefits will be taken away.

Americans are *not* against government but do tend to say they are. Robert J. Shapiro, a veteran of Budget and Finance Committee hearings in the Senate, offers the nice insight that while political liberals look to government to subsidize consumption of certain sorts, let us say food stamps, political conservatives are if anything more voracious in their demand for government subsidies for production, as in the farm program. In the first Reagan term, for example, farm subsidies rose from $2 billion (FY 1981) to $9 billion (FY 1984), an astonishing increase that went all but unnoticed, not least because farm subsidies are hidden in "off-budget" loan programs. Industrial subsidies are provided in the tax code under the heading of "Accelerated Cost Recovery System" and other such mysteries, which are, however, perfectly comprehensible to those who make use of them, and, to them, eminently defensible.

To say again, because it must be repeated if it is ever to be understood, the federal government grew larger under Mr. Reagan during his first term. It grew bigger in ways that those in office thought desirable; those who saw their notion of government provision shrink generally tended to accept the view that there was some great battle going on in Washington as to whether government should be reduced in size. Not really. The real conflict was over which aspects of government should grow.

In 1983, the total budget outlays of the federal government reached 23.1 percent of the gross national product, the highest level in the peacetime history of the Republic. Defense, interest payments, Social Security, and Medicare took most of this. All other federal outlays accounted for only 7.9 percent of GNP, and these were dropping back toward the range (6 percent or so) of the early 1960s, which is to say before the Great Society period. No matter that the President desired that this sector of the budget drop back. He also desired and actively pressed for greater defense outlays, which he increased somewhat, and by doubling the national debt, brought about a phenomenal increase in interest payments. (Two percent of GNP in 1980;

3.0 percent in 1984. Interest payments are now approaching half the outlays for defense. In passing, this probably represents the largest transfer of wealth from labor to capital in the history of our political economy.)

Out of this dichotomy, we observe the difficulties political liberals have persuading the public of their interest in economic growth; whilst conservatives struggle with the issue of "fairness." And yet intelligent conservatives concern themselves with fairness, if for no other reason than that the public does. Fairness is the point where the individualist ethos and collectivist ethos meet, and a White House task force sensibly asked (*before* the 1984 election), "Why Not 'Fairness' for Families?" In just this manner, the White House speech writers speak of the needs of families. Following the 1984 election, the *New York Times* interviewed the incoming head of the Democratic National Committee, asking of the election: "Was it more than just Reagan's skill? Was there also a period when the Democrats were seen to have been drifting away from the ideas of church, family, community?" The new chairman, Paul G. Kirk, Jr., answered: "I think that's true."

Is it possible that conservatives will think their way through to a "conservative vision of the welfare state" that is strongly oriented to family welfare? Is it possible that liberals might join and something of a center be reconstituted? Surely it is. But first we must address the proposition that where government has tried, government has only made matters worse; indeed, that it is government programs that have brought about the present "alarming rate of family disintegration."

This requires in the first instance that the argument of Charles Murray's *Losing Ground* be addressed. It is perhaps not fair to the author that his work be treated as a kind of court order enjoining the pursuit of social policy in the precincts of the U.S. Capitol, but it *is* proclaimed as having just such consequences. "For make no mistake," writes George Gilder, himself a formidable critic of welfare programs, "Murray has unleashed the most devastating sustained attack ever made against the welfare state."

Meg Greenfield's report is accurate. Inside the beltway, where conservative forces now preside (much as it may discomfit them), the thesis of *Losing Ground* prevails; certainly in the executive, and subtly elsewhere. Occasional echoes of the 1960s are heard: educators rediscover early-childhood education; doctors rediscover hunger. They are not listened to. The White House Task Force on Families begins its report with Murray's work and ends with it.

Early in 1985 the *New York Times* referred to the book as "this year's budget-cutters' bible," and in truth the Reagan budget sent to Congress in that season fitted well enough with the conclusions of *Losing Ground*: abolish the Job Corps, cut child nutrition programs, tighten AFDC still further. This had been going on. Between 1980 and 1985, while total federal outlays increased 21 percent in constant dollars, education outlays dropped almost a third. But now these measures were being proposed as a way to *help*. As Murray put it, "We tried to provide for the poor and produced more poor instead. We tried to remove the barriers to escape from poverty, and inadvertently built a trap." Hence, dismantle the trap. A *peripeteia*: a sudden reversal of fortunes. The propositions of the 1960s were all of a sudden turned on their heads.

First an assertion; then an acknowledgment. Murray is not so much to be answered as to be explained. This can be done with no injury to anyone; nor should any be intended. It is essential at the outset to acknowledge that he has written a responsible, meticulous work. He is manifestly concerned with the well-being of the persons he writes about and is convinced that existing government programs lead to self-destructive behavior. He writes as a former liberal, describing himself in an interview in the *Washington Times* as "a Kennedy Democrat who voted for Lyndon Johnson" (which would have been his first Presidential election). He believes, to cite the *Washington Times* interview, that "U.S. policy toward the poor took a fundamentally wrong turn during LBJ's tenure, and that the people who have suffered most have been those the new programs were supposed to benefit—poor Americans, especially inner-city blacks."

There is a significant subset of such persons with experiences similar to Murray's working on issues of social policy just now. (In the preface to his book [1984], Murray acknowledges the assistance of a friend in the Office of Management and Budget "who sees a common purpose in his civil rights work in Mississippi in the 1960s and his efforts to cut social programs in the 1980s.") The author graduated with honors from Harvard and received a Ph.D. from the Massachusetts Institute of Technology before spending six years in Thailand, first as a Peace Corps volunteer. From 1974 to 1981 he was a senior scientist, later chief scientist, at the American Institutes for Research (AIR), a nonprofit social-science research organization.

His field was evaluation research. He was, writes Gilder, "a sympathetic professional evaluator of the results of Great Society programs. . . ." As such, we may fairly assume he ran into Rossi's Iron Law. It is an experience that rather sets persons apart, especially, as was often the case in academic settings, when negative research findings were often met with great hostility. (In the 1960s a young sociologist arrived to do graduate work at Harvard. He had been much involved with student activists at the University of California at Berkeley and found Cambridge politically congenial. He had an unusual gift for mathematical sociology and was a valued member of the faculty seminar on the Coleman Report that took up the academic year 1967–68. The time came, however, when he published the results of his first field research. He had learned, to his own regret if not dismay, that a voluntary busing program appeared to do little whatever for student achievement or racial harmony and might have worsened both. His university career thus came to an end. In 1982 he ran for Congress in southern California as a Reagan Republican.) I believe the generalization is possible that a sensitive person beginning a professional career in the social sciences in the 1970s could easily have come to the judgment that conservatives—some conservatives—kept to higher standards than did their adversaries. Murray especially notes the encouragement of Irving Kristol in getting on with his work.

Let us also acknowledge the tradition in which Murray writes. In a review of the book, Leslie Lenkowsky, who has made a particular study of the similarities and differences between British and American welfare policies, notes that from the time of the Elizabethan Poor Law of 1601 "those concerned with social policy have wrestled with a troubling dilemma: how to aid the poor without encouraging lasting financial dependency." Lenkowsky cites Tocqueville's 1835 memoir on pauperism: "Any measure which establishes legal charity on a permanent basis and gives it an administrative form thereby creates an idle and lazy class."[2] He could have added the passage from Glazer with which I ended *The Politics of a Guaranteed Income*: "In its effort to deal with the breakdown of . . . traditional structures . . . social policy tends to encourage their further weakening. There is, then, no sea of misery against which we are making headway. Our efforts to deal with distress themselves increase distress."

Or this from Plutarch's life of Coriolanus: "For it was well and truly said that the first destroyer of the liberties of a people is he who first gave them bounties and largesses. At Rome the mischief seems to have stolen secretly in. . . ."

The argument will not end; the suspicion is too real. On the other hand, the question presents itself: How do we know? Causality in the social sciences is elusive. It is at most a matter of correlation, and correlation is not causality. Yet there are data. In France today, a century and a half after Tocqueville wrote, is there a distinct "idle and lazy class"? Not that we hear of. (It is said there was such a class prior to the Revolution, but this was called the aristocracy and accounts differ.) The contemporary French are said to take four weeks' vacation. But this is not idleness; it often appears to be just the opposite. As for Glazer's "sea of misery," is it the case we make *no* progress? From thirty years of friendship, I know that were I to ask him just how sure we can be that those "traditional structures" both existed and worked well, he would reply that that is indeed a question to be considered. Writing in the *Tocqueville Review* on the specific subject of recent changes in family patterns, William J. Goode (1985) puts the matter plainly enough:

> Social science has not created a genuine theory of social change, and I assert it will not do so in any foreseeable future. A true theory of social change is not merely a prophecy, not even one based on robust data about what causes change at present. A theory of social change specifies those causes to be sure, but it must also state that Phases B and C must occur after Phase A, and will do so under definable conditions, and at precise times.

Evolutionary theory had unsuccessfully attempted to explain the past, while "Marxism and its offshoot industrialization theory" had made various predictions about the future. "Unfortunately," Goode concludes, "history has not been kind to any of our social science predictions about futures." Much less can a work such as Murray's claim to account for the present.

Hence to the puzzle of *Losing Ground.* Trained to methodological rigor, the author goes through a period of testing the propositions implicit in various social programs and finds hypotheses unproved or disproved. He thereupon proceeds to quite breathtaking propositions of his own without adducing any evidence, nor yet allowing that in the absence of evidence we must proceed cautiously indeed. His evaluation of recent welfare policy involves a "thesis of infection." Thus he writes of the effect on social conventions of means-tested welfare benefits, such as food stamps, which appeared in some profusion during the Great Society period:

> The working people who made little money lost the one thing that enabled them to claim social status. For the first time in American history, it became socially acceptable within poor communities to be unemployed, because working families too were receiving welfare. Over a period of years, such changes in the rules of the economic game caused status conventions to flip completely in some communities.

To which the first response has got to be: Who says? Where do we learn that? Oscar Lewis spent a lifetime enquiring into questions of this sort and never quite satisfied himself. Hence: How does Mr. Murray know? The answer is that he does not. He may be right. But he has not proved anything.

Nor has he much addressed the data. The welfare explosion, and it was that, which has been a subject of such concern, took place in the 1960s. In that decade the number of families receiving AFDC increased 181 percent, while the number of children in AFDC families increased 168 percent. (The overall number of children in that decade increased only 8 percent.) In the 1970s, however, while the number of AFDC families increased 68 percent, the number of children receiving AFDC benefits increased only 19 percent. (The overall number of children fell 9 percent in the decade.) As regards welfare dependency, the change happened once, in the 1960s, and has simply not been reversed. As for the notion of any great explosion in welfare spending in the 1970s, neither can that be sustained. (We have noted the decline in the real value of AFDC benefits.) The increases took place in social-insurance programs that touch the poor least. Reviewing the data, David Ellwood and Lawrence Summers (1984) of Harvard University declare: "We are led to reject out of hand the increasingly fashionable view that poverty programs are the source of poverty problems." Again our attention turns to family change. Ellwood and Summers compress the matter nicely:

> Since 1972, the fraction of all children who were living in a female headed household jumped quite dramatically, from 14% to almost 20%. During that same period, the fraction of all children who were in homes collecting AFDC held almost constant at 12%. The figures are even more dramatic for blacks. Between 1972 and 1980 the number of black children in female headed families rose nearly 20%. The number of black children on AFDC actually fell by 5%!

If AFDC were pulling families apart and encouraging the formation of single parent families, it is very hard to understand why the number of children on the program would remain constant throughout the period in our history when family structures changed the most.

At this point the reader might well be confused and more than a little wary. Does anyone agree on anything? The answer is yes. On some things. Let us at this point introduce an exhibit, as lawyers might say. In the spring of 1985 Rudolph G. Penner, director of the Congressional Budget Office, appeared before the Subcommittee on Public Assistance and Unemployment Compensation of the Committee on Ways and Means of the House of Representatives. The hearings concerned children in poverty. In the manner of Washington officials, Dr. Penner brought with him prepared testimony and also a briefing book, in which possible or probable questions are posed with accompanying answers. Penner—a highly regarded economist and, what is perhaps in this context important to state, a Republican—was perfectly capable of improvising his own responses, but it is a courtesy to the committee to have as many things as possible written down in advance. Here, then, the inevitable question about welfare and the prepared response of a conservative government official.

Q. Critics contend that welfare programs have significant work disincentives that discourage recipients from taking jobs or from working as many hours as they otherwise would. Would you comment on this issue?

A. Yes. Welfare affects recipients' willingness to work in
   three ways.

First, families must satisfy eligibility criteria in order to
qualify for benefits. These may include some form of
work requirement—such as workfare or work registra-
tion—in which case there is a work incentive. On the
other hand, eligibility criteria may limit allowable work
or income—for example, families qualify for AFDC-UP
only if the primary worker is employed for fewer than
100 hours per month—creating a work disincentive. Income limits, especially when there is a notch, can also
affect a family's willingness to work.

Second, because welfare benefits increase a family's income, the family may choose to spend less time working
than otherwise. The transfer income means they need
not work as much in order to have a given level of total
income.

Finally, because welfare benefits are reduced as earnings
rise, recipients' gains from working an additional hour
are less than their wage rate—less by the amount benefits
are reduced. Since the net gain from working is lower,
recipients may choose to work fewer hours. For example,
if a family with $8,000 in earnings and getting food
stamps were to earn an additional $100, its food stamp
allotment would be reduced by up to $24, it would pay
at least $11 in additional income tax and $7 in additional
payroll tax, and its EITC [Earned Income Tax Credit]
would be cut by $12. The net effect would be to increase

its net income by $46, relative to its not earning the additional $100. The implicit tax rate of 54 percent would be a significant work disincentive.

In sum, there appear to be work incentives and work disincentives associated with the receipt of public welfare, but they appear at the margin, where some will work somewhat more hours and others somewhat fewer hours.

Yet what is any of this compared with the elemental ecology of work opportunities? It would appear that between 1979 and 1985, while 8.3 million jobs were added to the economy, the number of full-time jobs held by teenagers fell nearly 30 percent. Certain jobs simply are no longer there, while the people who once held them are. Allow me to witness this with more than statistics. New York is the city I know best. I was raised there and worked in such jobs. I would not wish to exaggerate. I joined the navy at age seventeen, toward the end of World War II. My working life in this regard was not long. And yet I did work in those factories, warehouses, piers. I know the persons I worked alongside. Such persons are still there; the jobs are not.

Social-welfare spending *does* have effects: Social Security probably reduces saving *somewhat*; unemployment insurance probably lengthens periods of unemployment *somewhat*; AFDC probably leads to more single-parent households *somewhat*. Any persevering reader of Dollard's *Caste and Class in a Southern Town* (1937) will learn of the "gains" of caste subservience in the antebellum South. But the main lesson of enquiry is that behavior is hard to explain and harder yet to modify. In this sense *Losing Ground* is not at all a break with the past. It merely continues the practice in Washington of making large assertions with no foundations. HEW Secretary Joseph Califano knew that welfare "breaks up families"; so does Dr. Murray. I don't. I wish we knew more; I fear we don't.

In response to various criticisms, including some of the above, Murray in the Fall 1985 issue of the *Political Science Quarterly* wrote that he had examined the experience of the last thirty years of social policy and had found "a variety of phenomena that demand explanation." He had put forth explanations consistent with what is known (i.e., hypotheses). "But to prove that I was right or wrong, or partly-right, or to demonstrate what the alternative 'truth' is, social science will have to explore questions that it has neglected." Agreed. Peace.

Still, there is no need to forget what we *did* know. In 1985 Murray told a symposium called "Lessons from the Great Society" that the "turns for the worse" which his book describes "were more pronounced than we had any reason to expect they should be." There was "no basis historically," he continued, "to predict the kinds of dramatic changes for the worse that did, in fact, occur." This is simply not so. Murray's work is concerned primarily with the growth of an urban minority underclass. *But that is precisely what I did predict in 1965, using data series that ended in 1964, before any of the events that he asserts have brought about these "turns for the worse."* It could well be that the predictions made in 1965 were not warranted, that I saw trends which did not as yet exist and only subsequently came about. Very well, but prove *that*. A personal, subjective judgment is that these realities, present or in prospect, throw people off. Thus the article denouncing the study that appeared in the *Nation* in 1965 stated that I had made "stupefying" assertions about minority crime rates. The rates were true; it was the *Nation*'s reviewer, William Ryan, who was stupefied. In a paper presented to a 1982 colloquium sponsored by the School of Welfare of the University of California at Berkeley and by the Bay Area Black United Fund, Jewelle Taylor Gibbs reported that in 1980 "black youth committed 51% of the violent juvenile crime in the U.S." and that the previous year "15% of all black adolescents in the 15–19 age group were arrested. . . ." These are grim numbers and can be disorienting.

If the response of those such as Ryan in 1965 to the data was essentially nonrational, I believe it can be shown that in Murray's case the response is nonlinear. Once again, it comes to this: *Losing Ground* attributes developments that trouble the author to government actions that mostly began *after* these developments had commenced as clearly recognizable statistical trends. It may be argued that these government actions intensified these developments, but the data are not at all conclusive.

There are things we *have* learned. In "Family Structure and Living Arrangements Research: Summary of Findings" (March 1984), Mary Jo Bane and David Ellwood present an exhaustive series of cross correlations examining various family patterns and the impact of the AFDC program. The existing welfare program provides in this regard a kind of natural experiment. Each of the fifty states has a somewhat different program, as do Puerto Rico and Guam. Benefits vary enormously. At middecade a family of four can now collect $120 a month in Mississippi, in other states $600 or more. And the effects? With one large exception, they could find no effects:

> Differences in welfare benefit levels do not appear to be the primary cause of variation in family structure across states, or over time. Largely unmeasurable differences in culture, attitudes or expectations seem to account for most of the differences in birth rates to unmarried women and in divorce and separation patterns among families with children.

In Minnesota, benefits are high; divorce rates and unmarried births are low. It is the other way around in Mississippi. And so their analyses go, taking us back rather in the direction of William Graham Sumner's on the power of folkways over stateways.

The one "dramatic impact" they determine is that of benefit levels on living arrangements. In low-benefit states, a young mother not living with a husband is very likely to live in the home of a parent. In high-benefit states, such women are more likely to live independently. They suggest that between 1960 and 1982 about one-third of the increase in female-headed households resulted from an increase in the number of single mothers who live independently. Thus some statistical trends may appear more troubling than is the case.

Ellwood and Bane find an increase in the proportion of black women between age eighteen and forty-four who have never married: from 27 percent in 1970 to 44 percent in 1982. White proportions increase also. They note: "The percentage employed of young black men has been deteriorating rapidly in the past decade, at the same time that marriage rates have been falling." They suggest it is "quite plausible" that the one influences the other. But: "As an explanation for the dramatic changes in family structure, welfare benefits are largely impotent."

The Panel Study of Income Dynamics, a sample of five thousand American families conducted by the Survey Research Center at the University of Michigan, has produced important findings. As analyzed by Greg J. Duncan and his associates (1984), in the decade 1969–78 a quarter (24.4 percent) of American families were poor for one or more years, but only 2.6 percent were "persistently poor," which is to say for eight or more years. As to the "near poor," if the official poverty line were raised by a quarter, a third (32.5 percent) of American families would have been poor sometime during this ten-year period. As to welfare, Duncan concludes "the system does not foster dependency." Half the families in the sample who received welfare did so for no more than two of the ten years. He characterizes welfare as "a kind of insurance . . . providing temporary assistance." And to take us back to the beginnings of the poverty program, he opens his chapter "The Dynamics of Poverty" with that passage from Matthew 26:11, "You have the poor among you always." All that has changed from the hearing room in the House of Representatives twenty years earlier is the Bible translation; Duncan used the New English Bible, while Congressman William H. Ayres had quoted the King James Version.

It may be that the Michigan group understates the doggedness of dependency. Ellwood and Bane find that most women who go on AFDC do so for short spells, but the bulk of AFDC expenditures "are accounted for by women who have spells of eight years or more." A third of women who end one spell of AFDC "return for another spell." Most importantly, "three-fourths of all spells of AFDC began with a relationship change whereby a female-headed family with children was created." Only a fraction, 12 percent, could be traced to earnings decreases. Again to the thesis of 1965, the previous relationship between dependency and income and employment just isn't quite there any longer.

One of the persistent difficulties in assessing the impact of the Great Society period is that for all the sound and fury—not all that much happened. In the study by James T. Patterson cited previously, it is estimated that in its period of greatest independence and activity, the late 1960s, *total* expenditures by the Office of Economic Opportunity came to about $50 to $70 per poor person in the United States. The big increases in social spending of that time were associated with the maturing of the Social Security system and one major addition to that system. This latter was the establishment of health-care insurance for the elderly and the dependent, known respectively as Medicare and Medicaid. These large innovations in social policy took place quite independently of the hullabaloo at OEO. They were in the main the work of a small group of public servants—Wilbur J. Cohen, Robert M. Ball, and others—who had been involved with the establishment of Social Security in 1935 and were still at it three decades later. Health insurance had been on their agenda for years. In the months following the assassination of John F. Kennedy they saw their opportunity, and they took it. The legislation—Titles XVIII and XIX of the Social Security Act—was adopted with little exertion and less analysis. This is to say that the cost estimates were absurdly low, done more or less on the back of an envelope. The genius of the sponsors of Medicare and Medicaid was that having quietly waited thirty years for their "moment" to come again, they seized it.

The report to President Roosevelt of the Committee on Economic Security was transmitted by Secretary of Labor Frances Perkins and her cabinet associates (plus Harry L. Hopkins) on January 15, 1935. (Would the President's Task Force on Manpower Conservation had had as specific a proposal!) On January 17 the bill was introduced in the Senate by Robert F. Wagner of New York. It was signed by the President seven months later on August 14. The New Deal soon came to an end, and no equivalent moment of legislative opportunity reappeared until 1965, when about the same sequence was followed with health insurance. As with earlier provisions of Social Security, the health-care entitlements soon dwarfed any mere antipoverty program getting along from year to year on the annual appropriations.

With respect to welfare dependency, Medicaid posed a

genuine question. By 1965, it was clear enough that the AFDC program no longer resembled anything like the widow's program contemplated by the original Aid to Dependent Children provision of the 1935 act. If welfare *did* break up families, Medicaid was going to add a large additional incentive: complete medical insurance. By 1983, total direct cash payments to AFDC families would be $13.6 billion. Medicaid payments would provide these families more than half again that amount, $8 billion, as in-kind payments, averaging $409 per year for children and $884 for adults.

Now then: *Did* Medicaid increase welfare dependency? Had we been interested in this possibility (almost no one was in 1965) we could in theory have devised an experiment. One group in the population would receive Medicaid; another, the control group, would not. After a time we would compare the behavior of the two groups. But of course this is only theoretically possible. Congress cannot provide welfare benefits as a legal entitlement to one group of citizens and deny them to another.

Even so, an experiment took place. States *choose* to participate in certain Social Security programs. As it happens, for some seventeen years Arizona chose not to participate in Medicaid. The program began in 1966; Arizona entered in 1982. By contrast, neighboring New Mexico entered the program almost at the outset. And the results in these adjoining states, with their matched populations? Over the fifteen years, 1967–82, the number of AFDC families in New Mexico increased 127 percent; in Arizona 121 percent.* Where, then, is the Great Society effect on welfare dependency?

It would be mindless to dismiss any "welfare effect" on the incidence of welfare dependency. There were many rule changes in the period just after 1965, some legislative, some administrative. Almost invariably these made it easier to obtain welfare—easier to cheat—and infrequently increased benefit levels. Some years ago, Heather L. Ross and Isabel V. Sawhill (1975) found that increasing the level of welfare benefits produced a "modest upward influence on the proportion of female-headed families." But this line of research has not produced any evidence whatever to account for the magnitude of the change in female-headed and dependent families in the past twenty years or so. (To anticipate somewhat, the Reagan administration obtained many new restrictions on the AFDC program in the Omnibus Budget Reconciliation Act of 1981. The number of AFDC families thereupon dropped in 1982, only to begin

---

* Over the period 1967 to 1982, the number of AFDC families in the U.S. rose more rapidly, by 191 percent, than in Arizona and New Mexico. The relatively low AFDC need standards (which govern program eligibility) prevailing in Arizona and New Mexico and the erosion in those standards over time are likely causes for this differential.

In 1970, the AFDC need standard for a four-person family in Arizona was 8 percent below the same standard for the median U.S. state; in New Mexico, the need standard was 27 percent below that of the median state. By 1985, the need standards in Arizona and New Mexico had fallen even further behind; Arizona's need standard fell to a level 42 percent below the median state's, and New Mexico's standard fell to 36 percent below.

rising again in 1983. Slightly but, you might say, willfully.)

I return to the issues I raised in 1965 and the reaction. I had proposed a national response to the growing problems of low-status black families, and I had a President with me—sort of with me. But then everybody got mad and the subject was dropped. Had the national government attempted a sustained policy response, there might have been some effect. Had this response concentrated on male employment, and had it succeeded in those terms, there might have been a more general effect. I do not know, and there is no way to know.

But in the event, something very different happened. Or so I believe, on the testimony of Mary Jo Bane, now executive deputy commissioner of the New York State Department of Social Services and a tenacious and inspired scholar. In 1984 a conference called "Poverty and Policy: Retrospect and Prospects" was held at Williamsburg, Virginia. The object was to review the experience of the 1960s and 1970s, and to consider what lessons might be learned for the 1980s and 1990s. In a 1984 paper on household composition and poverty, Bane began with the feminization of poverty: in the early 1980s, about half the poor were women living alone or members of households headed by women. She traced this development and concluded "that poverty policy may have worked reasonably well for some groups of poor women, but that it may well have been a disaster for chronically poor blacks." Starting with the 1965 report there was, first, denial, then encounter, and, finally, *flight*. In a section headed "The Roots of Social Abandonment," she asked what had brought about "a situation in which the better off among the poor or potentially poor are better served by social policy than the worse off." It could be old American tendencies "to help the well off or to discriminate against blacks." But it could also be that in contrast, say, to mailing out checks to the elderly, "the problems of getting the persistently poor out of poverty, in contrast, seems to be incredibly hard to solve." She continues:

> One reason for giving up on (or never trying) the educational and employment efforts advocated by the war on poverty is that they seem to be nearly impossible to make work. The programs that do seem to work for the chronically poor, like supported work, are very expensive and their successes have been small. The programs that work . . . also seem to require a degree of discipline and motivation that liberals have been unwilling to enforce and clients to demand; it is, after all, easier for both sides to slack off.

˙ That, in my view, is about what happened during these years. Government did not transform the behavior of those in greatest difficulty; it pretty much left them be. Behavior that was already more than sufficiently self-destructive simply went forward, with the consequences growing more pronounced—which is the normal progression of self-destructive behavior. Not only did we do nothing, we learned nothing. This must be touched upon. Bane notes that the controversy over the black family study "led to the avoidance by scholars and policy makers of the whole problem, which has gotten steadily and dramatically worse since the time of the publication of the report."

In the mid-1980s, an almost sudden realization of this arose among black writers and commentators. The poor had been terribly let down. Persons with very different agendas had been pleased to come forth with helpful nostrums about "alternative" life-styles and "healthful" adaptations to changing times and such drivel. When reality turned out to be so much more harsh, those who had prettified it simply departed. In the spring of 1985, Eleanor Holmes Norton wrote in the *New York Times* with a touch of tartness: "Some argue persuasively that the female-headed family is an adaptation that facilitates coping with hardship and demographics. This seems undeniable as an explanation, but unsatisfactory as a response. Are we willing to accept an adaptation that leaves the majority of black children under the age of 6—the crucial foundation years of life—living in poverty?"

Weeks earlier William Raspberry asked in a *Washington Post* column: "Will the Underclass Be Abandoned?" America's black middle class, he wrote, was approaching a fork in the road: they "will either undertake an unprecedented and enormously difficult salvage operation—or else run for [their] lives." Yet, in another column he asked what could be done. The concerns and conditions Martin Luther King, Jr., had set forth twenty years earlier had been ignored, and now what? Raspberry's words are a *cri de coeur*:

Those of us who were the beneficiaries of the earlier civil-rights movement—whose middle-class attitudes of academic preparation and hard work enabled us to take advantage of the opportunities that movement made available—have not been able to devise a comparable breakthrough for the growing underclass.

The youngsters most in need of help seem least ready for it. They lack the basic skills and, more dismayingly, the basic attitudes that would make them attractive even as entry-level employees. They don't know how to seek the help they need, and worse, they positively frighten those who feel the urge to offer help.

We are helpless, idea-less witnesses to a near-total social breakdown. The concerned professionals who could command the resources don't know what to do. Members of the youngsters' own families, who at an earlier time might have helped them learn the attitudes that would help them secure the special help they need, often don't have the appropriate attitudes themselves, having spent most of their lives outside the formal job structure. In a growing number of instances, their households hardly qualify as families at all.

Helpless, idea-less witnesses to a near-total social breakdown? In a sense, yes. But not solitary witnesses. A large, to my mind, defining development was that by the mid-1980s, it was clear that family disorganization had become a general feature of the American population and not just an aspect of a frequently stigmatized and appropriately sensitive minority community.

In 1965 I could state that "the United States is approaching a new crisis in race relations," because the number of "nonwhite" families with a female head had reached 21 percent. By 1984 the census would report that for white families with children this proportion had reached nearly 20 percent. Nineteen sixty had been 9 percent, 1970 10 percent; then, of a sudden, double. In 1984 single-parent families with children accounted for more than one-quarter (26 percent) of all family groups (white, black, Hispanic, et al.) compared with 22 percent in 1980 and only 13 percent in 1970. Since 1970 the number of single-parent families had increased 124 percent, while the number of all families with children increased only 12 percent and the number of married-couple families with children actually declined 4 percent. Women headed 89 percent of all one-parent families in 1984. All this is not to dismiss the black-white disparity. In 1984, 59 percent of all black family groups with children were one-parent situations, as against the near 20 percent among whites. This is a three-to-one ratio. *The Negro Family* recorded that the ratio had been somewhat less than two-to-one in 1950, somewhat more than that in 1960. The gap has widened. Even so, what was a crisis condition for the one group in 1960 is now the general condition. (The Associated Press writes: "The year 1985 may be remembered as the year of the missing child." By far the greater number of such children, 100,000 or more, are abducted by a parent.)

The future looks to be much like the recent past. The Population Division of the Bureau of the Census has for some time been projecting family composition.[3] No exceptional claims are made, save that the work is professional, which is to say cautious, and internally consistent.

In overall terms, by the end of the century we project that about three-quarters of American families will be of the "traditional" sort, whereas in 1960 nearly nine of ten families could be so described. In less than two generations the proportion of families headed by single persons will have doubled. Again, we can assume a good deal of churning, with children more and more likely to spend some portion of their childhood in single-parent households.

In the final two decades of the century we project the number of families will increase from 59.5 million to 72.5 million, which is to say a net of 13 million families. But of these additional households, only 5.9 million are expected to be "traditional" husband-wife families. Female-headed families will account for 5.8 million of the net increase, and male-headed families for 1.3 million. Put another way, in the period 1980–2000 the number of female-headed families will increase at more than five times the rate of husband-wife families. Family households headed by males with no wife present will increase at some six times of rate of the traditional sort. Black-white differentials will persist but probably moderate. The black illegitimacy ratio, for example, is almost certainly an artifact of a declining birth rate in which higher status groups take the lead.

These projections suggest that the issue of family welfare will continue to make claims for attention in the decades ahead. If, as seems evident, we are in a conservative period in social policy, the family "trends" between now and the end of the century ought to engage the concern of groups committed to and proselytizing on behalf of "traditional" arrangements. A. James Reichley (1984) has persuasively contended that the political shifts of the 1980s have come about largely because of the entry into conservative politics of white evangelical Protestants—the Revolt of the Evangelicals, he calls it—in the aftermath of Supreme Court decisions on abortion and school prayer and a shift to conservative politics by Roman Catholics brought on by the same events. These are political sensibilities amenable to consideration of social policies that affect family structure and welfare, as well as family values. The depths of such sensibilities are easily missed. The general suggestion may be offered that the "interest-group liberalism" of traditional Democrats met with rejection, in considerable measure, because it did not accommodate itself to a changed political reality in which intensely interested elements in the electorate had no *self*-interests. (Without hesitation I would state that of all the groups which appeal for the attention and support of a senator from New York, the one that by far is the most broadly based in the electorate and least self-interested—save as the public confirmation of personal moral beliefs is a matter of self-interest—is the Right to Life movement.)

Yet social welfare concerns are legitimately part of liberal tradition also. When Mario M. Cuomo became governor of New York in 1983, he proclaimed "The Family of New York" as the theme of his administration. At the same time, the prospects for family dysfunction in years ahead also invite a renewed concern by political liberals for whom such matters are indicators of general social dysfunction, and who generally make the case for a public-policy response. Just possibly these otherwise competing and antagonistic factions might find common ground in family policy.

Granted, this is not easy to see. Gilbert Y. Steiner has much the better case in his contention that nothing approaching a coherent family policy can be attained through the American political process for the simple reason that family welfare means too many conflicting things to too many conflicting groups. "Many Causes with Many Votaries" is the title he gives to the concluding chapter of his work *The Futility of Family Policy*.

Steiner's study is largely a critique of the Carter administration's failure to achieve any of the goals it promised in this area. Here President Carter was unique. Alone among Presidential candidates, recent or remote, Carter made "the American family . . . in trouble" a strong and recurring theme of his campaign. Steiner describes it this way: "Without limiting the judgment of a 'steady erosion and weakening of our families' to any ethnic or economic group, he stated his intention 'to construct an administration that will reverse the trends we have seen toward the breakdown of the family in our country.'" Yet in the end he accomplished nothing. Worse, he made the case that nothing could be accomplished. In the closing month of the 1976 Presidential campaign he told a meeting of the National Conference of Catholic Charities that one of his first steps upon becoming President would be to convene a "White House Conference on the American Family." Califano, his first secretary of HEW, was put in charge, and three years later a sort of conference took place—on "Families." It had proved impossible to reach agreement among Democrats of the kind appointed or preferred by the Carter administration as to whether there was a social norm that could be described as simply "the American Family."

Much of this may be ascribed to the general haplessness of the Carter administration. By some attraction of opposites, this decent Southern evangelical politician filled his administration with persons not just incapable of political thought, but often as not contemptuous of what was politic. Even so, Mr. Carter cared about family issues and understood the relevance of government to them. His Vice President, Walter F. Mondale, had made family policy part of his own agenda during the early 1970s in the Senate and had given some currency to the notion that government economic and social programs should be accompanied by a Family Impact Statement modeled on the Environmental Impact Statement that had been made a part of public-works programs in that period. Thus in 1977, for the first time in American history, an administration came to office proclaiming the importance of family policy and presumably intent on putting one in place.

Right off, in August 1977, Carter proposed welfare reform—the Program for Better Jobs and Income—a guaranteed income along the lines President Nixon had proposed in 1969. He gave extraordinary personal attention to the details of the proposal. But it quite eluded him that the very fact that so much attention was required and that there was so much detail meant the proposal could never make its way through Congress. Nixon's experience had shown that. In any event, that sort of initiative was a thing of the political past. Henry Aaron, who at HEW helped with the measure, describes it as "stillborn."[4] The Committee on Ways and Means in the House of Representatives, where such a measure would have had to originate, never so much as held a hearing of its own on the President's plan.

In winter and spring of 1978 the Senate Subcommittee on Public Assistance did hold hearings, trying to be helpful. But we didn't much help. Steiner describes the opening hearing in which Califano appeared and, in Steiner's words, commenced his "routine intonation" that welfare—the AFDC program—breaks up families. I asked for particulars; might it be that HEW knew something we did not know? He had none; there were none. A serious public official, he was even so inaccessible to the thought that by now such an assertion had to be supported. As Steiner recounts the occasion, I asked the secretary, "How do you know?" He responded that Walter Reuther had so testified before a subcommittee chaired by then-Senator Mondale. Steiner notes that Mondale's Subcommittee on Children and Youth held its hearings on the family in 1973. Reuther had died in 1970.

This, sadly, is significant. At this point in time, there was simply no excuse for the head of the cabinet department responsible, to the degree anyone is responsible, for the welfare of families not to have mastered a basic brief on his or her programs. The more so, if the programs were to be described as doing harm: breaking up families, bankrupting businesses, killing off songbirds, whatever. How's that again, Mr. Secretary? Yet Democratic officeholders operated under a near-opposite imperative. It was best not to know too much about welfare, about families, about the explosive issues of race that could so easily be touched off. The permanent government had learned to withhold information that would be unsettling or downright unwelcome. At the time Mr. Califano appeared to testify on behalf of a guaranteed income, the negative results of the Seattle/ Denver experiments were known in Washington. The Seattle/Denver Income Maintenance Experiment (SIME/ DIME) was the last in a series of four large-scale income-maintenance experiments undertaken in the late 1960s and early 1970s to measure the effects of cash transfers on such factors as labor-force participation and marital stability. But it was most unlikely that the head of the department that financed the experiments knew the results; at all events Califano made no mention of them. (The subcommittee, which is to say the general public, learned nothing until one afternoon in November 1978 when John Cogan, a young economist from Stanford, came to testify and told us, "They won't tell you this," but it hadn't worked.)

In the end I asked the secretary to outline the administration's current thinking on family policy—a matter obviously vital in welfare reform. He gave the committee his answer in writing: "The Administration, to date, has established no formal, overall 'family policy,' but a great deal of attention has been focused on the interaction of programs and proposed legislation with an impact on families."

Carter departed in 1981, but things were "left undone,"

and a shadow was cast over much that he had promised five years earlier. In 1976, the Democratic platform committed the party to federal assumption of the costs of the AFDC program and the establishment of a uniform national payment. It was not clear whether Carter ever accepted this idea as a candidate, and he never proposed it while President. Here again the mystery of those years. The President would slave over a negative tax with as many moving parts as a Rolls-Royce engine but have nothing to do with a proposal of elemental simplicity that the Social Security Administration could administer with one microchip. In any event, the commitment was repeated in the 1980 platform. In January 1981, the outgoing President sent up his departing budget. The simplest fidelity would have led him to include the AFDC proposal. He did not. I questioned his domestic advisor and was told that it had been decided that to do so would be to give the incoming Reagan administration "an easy cut."

And yet the issue persists. With the 1980 election the new Republican majority in the Senate abolished the Subcommittee on Public Assistance, and the new administration at times seemed bent on abolishing public assistance itself. A fair number of changes were made in the AFDC program, all tending to make it more difficult to get on the rolls or stay on the rolls, as the new administration would put it. And yet the "rolls" have not gone down, while the poverty rate, however defined, has been going up.

Strictly in terms of cost, the Congressional Budget Office projects that AFDC expenditures will drop to 0.7 percent of total federal outlays by 1990. It had reached 1.6 percent of the budget in 1973. The Supplementary Security Income program is now almost as large.

The number of children in AFDC families passed the 8 million mark in 1976 but has since dropped back to about 7 million and stays there. (In December 1980, during the transition to the Reagan administration, the *Washington Post* suggested that indeed it would be almost worthwhile abolishing the program, "in order to be rid of this convenient scapegoat.")

But yet again another set of simplicities was defeated, or at least not vindicated. By 1984, as noted, a family-policy group was meeting regularly in the Reagan White House. After a lapse of nearly two decades, precisely the same subjects were under discussion once again. There is a normal temptation in any administration to blame predecessors. One seems to recall in the 1960s the notion that the Eisenhower years had somehow been repressive. By the 1980s the 1960s were seen as far too permissive. Thus from the cabinet paper: "Drug abuse and alcoholism among youth also flowered as the liberal welfare state fertilized America's social structure." But there was a continuity just as significant. Then, as now, reasonably experienced persons with informed views as to what kinds of things government seems to do well, or seems to be able to do at all, turned their attention away from tinkering with the welfare programs to questions of the distribution of income generally.

The difficulty for the newest group was that the Reagan administration had contrived the deficit as a more or less deliberate strategy to ensure that the Federal government would have no income to redistribute. In his first televised address to the nation as President, on February 5, 1981, sixteen days after taking office, Mr. Reagan said as much: "There were always those who told us that taxes couldn't be cut until spending was reduced. Well, you know, we can lecture our children about extravagance until we run out of voice and breath. Or we can cure their extravagance by simply reducing their allowance."

The budget deficits of the administration's first term were far in excess of anything planned or desired, but it was planned that a continuing, sizable-enough deficit would shift Congressional debate away from additions to government and toward a protracted, grinding debate as to where to cut and how much. The Reagan deficits basically involved a theory of government. Much as the Framers had contrived complex checks and balances to limit the powers of the national government with respect to the more elemental manifestations of sovereignty in an eighteenth-century government, the Reagan deficit was an institutional device to limit the activities of government in the areas of social policy that developed in the twentieth century. This strategy was abetted by the Congressional Budget and Impoundment Act of 1974, which Frank C. Ballance has described as "a well-intentioned reform for Congressional reconciliation of revenues and expenditures, [that] has spawned a time-consuming and complex budget process and forces accommodation in a way that has the greatest impact on the weakest programs."[5] Even had the Reagan administration changed its views on the existing welfare arrangements and tried to make them more generous, the deficit and the budget process would have prevented it. As for anything so grand as a guaranteed income, both the condition of the Treasury and the state of knowledge ruled it out altogether. In Aaron's summation, "the hypothesis that noncategorical welfare would increase family stability remain[ed] unsupported by empirical research. The contrary hypothesis ha[d] received official, if premature, support."[6]

And so attention turned to the tax system. This was in any event a normal disposition of the Reagan administration. On February 1, 1972, during his tenure as governor of California, Mr. Reagan had come to Washington to testify before the Senate Finance Committee. In opposition to the Family Assistance legislation (to repeat, a guaranteed income), he proposed instead a version of an earned income tax credit, whereby wage earners with incomes below the poverty level would be absolved of tax otherwise owed, in order to bring them up to (or nearer to) the poverty line. (Such at least was the subject of his written testimony; his spoken comments centered on waste, fraud, and abuse by AFDC families, and his success in reducing the rolls in California.) In his 1972 testimony Mr. Reagan contended that the proper federal response for poor families was reduced taxes:

Many fully employed families work for compensation which is insufficient to meet their minimum needs. This becomes more severe as the size of the family increases. Because they are fully employed, they are ineligible for the AFDC programs. Rather than create a new category of welfare recipients, it is proposed that the situation of such low-income families be improved by providing automatic exemptions from state and federal income taxes and an automatic rebate of social security taxes including the employer's contribution thereto. The solution concerning these families is to provide a better return for their efforts through such exemptions and rebates rather than place them on public relief unrelated to their work efforts and productivity.

Here is another of the anomalies of the American approach to social insurance. In 1975 a Democratic Congress and a Republican President, Gerald Ford, did much as Mr. Reagan proposed, enacting the Earned Income Tax Credit Act of that year. (The Senate had passed versions in 1972, 1973, and 1974, under the prodding of Senator Russell Long of Louisiana; he liked to call it a "Work Bonus.") Under the act, low-income working families with children can claim a tax credit or, if their income is low enough, receive a *cash payment* of up to $550 per year. By the 1980s between 6 and 7 million families were receiving benefits, which "cost" just under $2 billion a year. About one-third of this amount was received in the form of reduced taxes, two-thirds as cash payments. After all the controversy over the Family Assistance Plan, a recognizable negative income tax—the E.I.T.C.—was adopted almost without comment.

For that matter, the great "reform," as Richard P. Nathan observed at the time, was the transformation in the 1960s and 1970s of the Department of Agriculture food programs from a marginal activity distributing surplus commodities in unappetizing forms to a massive food-stamp program that routinely, and as a matter of entitlement, distributes this form of currency to some 6.5 million households (as of the first quarter 1984). This represents almost twice the 3.9 million households receiving AFDC payments at this time. To cite the census: "Among food stamp households, 69 percent had Medicaid coverage, 40 percent had children who received free or reduced-price school meals, 23 percent lived in public or subsidized rental housing, and 11 percent received benefits under the WIC [Women, Infants and Children] nutrition program."

This is the anomaly that confronts the policymaker or advocate. Family deterioration neither proceeds from nor responds to efforts at relief. In the circumstances, it appears best not even to try to be theoretical, much less "scientific." If a negative tax—an academic construct—disappoints, attention turns to the workaday real world of the tax system that actually exists.

Thus it was natural enough for the planners in the Reagan White House in 1984 to pursue the strategy the President had outlined in his testimony of the previous decade. Key data were supplied by Eugene Steuerle (1983), then of the American Enterprise Institute and now a Treasury official. The personal and dependent exemptions in the income tax were introduced in 1913 and 1917 respectively. Each taxpayer exempts from taxable income a certain amount for himself or herself and for each remaining member of the household: wife, husband, children. The "typical" tax return for a husband-wife family claims four exemptions. The dependent exemption is in this sense a children's allowance built into the tax code, much as AFDC payments are (and originally were solely) children's allowances built into the Social Security System. As noted, in 1948 the exemption was $600. Steuerle calculated that "if the personal exemption had been indexed for income growth since 1948—in other words, if the exemption were to offset the same percentage of per capita personal income today as it did in 1948—then it would equal . . . about $5,600 in 1984. . . ." (The $600 per-person exemption amounted on average to 42 percent of per capita personal income in 1948.) By 1984, however, the exemption had been increased to only $1,000. By another measure, if the exemption had been indexed by increases in the Consumer Price Index, the $600 exemption in 1948 would have been a $2,589 exemption in 1984. Steuerle concludes: "By any measure, this decline in the personal exemption has been the largest single change in the income tax in the postwar era."

This issue came up, as noted, in the *America* article in 1965: "The 'value' of the income-tax exemption for wives and children has steadily eroded since its present level was set in 1948." Then-recent tax cuts, I went on, "certainly have not improved, and may have further worsened the relative tax burden of poor families." In 1948 the median income for a family of four was $3,468, and the threshold for federal income taxes in 1948 was $2,667, being the $600 personal exemption (times four) plus the $267 standard deduction. This means that more than three-fourths of median family income in 1948 was exempt from federal tax. Was this not in effect a powerful national family policy?

It costs money to raise a family, and the federal government chose not to tax most of the income so required. This is no longer so. In 1983 the median income for a family of four was $29,184, and, according to the Joint Committee on Taxation, the federal income tax threshold had reached $8,783—which means that less than one-third of median family income was exempt.

It may well be that in more than three decades of respectable economic growth, median income grew faster than the costs of raising a family, but just as surely not that much faster. The point here is that the costs of raising a family no longer bear any relationship to the amount of income not subject to federal tax. This relationship is so askew that a poor family—not just of median income, but one below the poverty line—is subject to tax. In 1948 the poverty line for a family of four would have been $2,454, or some $200 below the income-tax threshold. In 1983 the poverty line was $10,166 for a family of four, but federal tax liability in that year began at $8,783. Two decades after the enactment of the Economic Opportunity Act, the federal government was *taxing* the poor at levels without equal in history. The Joint Committee on Taxation (1984) reported that the gap between the threshold for income-tax liability and the poverty level is growing. In 1984 the Income Statistics Branch of the Census Bureau analyzed federal taxation of poor Americans. They reported that in 1982, 7 percent of all households living below the poverty line—515,000 poor families—paid federal income taxes, three times the number of four years earlier. (In addition, 15 percent of all poor families paid some state income tax, and more than half of all households below the poverty line were paying Social Security taxes.)

What we see here is the "flattening" of the tax system. In 1948 the income tax was highly progressive, with marginal rates upwards of 80 percent on upper-income families (rising higher still, to 92 percent, in 1952) and with little or no tax whatever levied on low-income families. This slowly changed. Marginal rates came down, to 70 percent in the mid-1960s and 50 percent in 1982. Meanwhile, inflation pushed more and more low-income families into the taxable range, principally because the value of the personal and dependent exemption was not maintained. Meanwhile, the Social Security tax, which begins with the first dollar of earned income, rose steadily. In 1948, this tax claimed 1 percent of the first $3,000 of earnings; in 1984, seven percent (of the first $37,800). All told, combining federal income and Social Security taxes, an American family of median income in 1948 paid about 4.4 percent of its income to the federal government; by 1982, the federal government was claiming some 18 percent of the median family's income.

Has this change weakened families? Strengthened them? There is no way to say. We do, however, know something of the cost of raising children. Thomas J. Espenshade (1984) of the Urban Institute estimated that for a medium-status, four-person family, the average total expenditure to raise a child through age 18 is $82,400 (in 1981 dollars). The amount varies some by family status and is somewhat higher where the wife is employed, but the range is rather narrow, hovering about an average of not quite $4,600 per child per year. Mind, this is not a measure of need but of actual expenditure. Even so, it is suggestive to compare Steuerle's estimates with those of Espenshade. We learn that to maintain the value of the personal exemption of a generation past, by one measure, would call for approximately a $5,600 exemption at present. We learn that the average annual cost of raising a child is $4,600 at present. Can we conclude that in 1948 the cost of raising a child was automatically deducted from income? No, obviously not. Yet it might have been. The point is, is it not, that tax policy should extend to such questions. It does not now.

Credit, then, to the tax planners of the Reagan administration. In his 1985 State of the Union address, Mr. Reagan declared that tax reform would be a primary objective of his second term. The preceding November his Treasury Department issued a detailed proposal that along with other things would increase the personal exemption to $2,000. On further thought, partial credit. Treasury I, as it came to be known, a three-volume work entitled *Tax Reform for Fairness, Simplicity and Economic Growth*, promptly became the subject of much dispute. The basic strategy of the proposal was to eliminate provisions in the tax code that provide various kinds of exemptions or deductions, thus increasing revenue that in turn could be distributed to the general population through lower tax rates. Those whose taxes would rise naturally objected and just as naturally pressed to limit the increase in the personal deduction that, apart from rate reduction, was the single most costly change proposed. (Some $40 billion per year in income not taken from those with dependents, mainly families with children.)

At the higher echelons in the Treasury, the case for, say, a $1,500 personal deduction began to have appeal. The family-policy group in the White House intervened and in the end successfully, but not before being informed by a member of the subcabinet that "children are a consumption good" and that just possibly *no* deduction was in order.

And there it is. The view that "children are a consumption good" has crept into official thinking, and to the degree such thinking is reflected in policy, *that* is a *family policy*. Nothing but good can come from raising such assumptions to the level of general awareness.

At a first level, this is almost a simple exercise. Once a high Treasury official has stated the view that "children are a consumption good," we know—most of us know—that we do not think that and ought not. To be sure, we do not know the processes of social change well enough to be able confidently to predict them, far less to affect them. What we do know is what we generally value as a society and what generally we think is conducive to the things we value. We value self-sufficiency. We are offended by poverty. It follows that we should not tax individuals, much less families, to the point where they are officially poor and potentially dependent. We now do that. Would recent trends in family structure change if we stopped doing it or if we did it to a lesser degree? We do not know. But it is not necessary to know (and probably not possible). What is necessary is the willingness and ability to act in some coherent manner in accordance with some coherent objective. We can act if we can agree, and this is a matter on which we can agree. Do not tax people into poverty.

Do not tax them below their family's needs. We can further agree that in this matter we are not so much changing things as restoring what was once in place, remembering answers we once thought obvious. Is this not a common ground? A possible common ground? What else?

In addition to a restoring (and maintaining the importance) of the value of the personal and dependent exemptions for families with low incomes, there has got to be a better provision for those with little or none, which is to say AFDC families. In the 1960s and 1970s all the entitlement programs of the federal government were indexed against price inflation with the single exception of the entitlements of children. The consequences in the 1970s have been noted. The AFDC program, Title IV of the Social Security Act, should be brought into conformity with the other titles that provide cash benefits. The federal government should assume the full cost of the program, set a national standard, and index that standard for price changes. This is within our political capacity. The national Democratic party is at least on record in support of a measure to "federalize" welfare payments. As recently as 1972, the Republican party platform urged "uniform Federal payment standards for all welfare recipients." A national standard for AFDC payments, which is to say a uniform, national benefit level, would declare a genuine national concern for children. Its absence is the clearest example we have of national family policy that takes the form of denying policy.

The subject does not end there. The issue of dependency remains. In 1973 I began an account of the Family Assistance saga with a paragraph I would not know how to improve on:

> The issue of welfare is the issue of dependency. It is different from poverty. To be poor is an objective condition; to be dependent, a subjective one as well. That the two circumstances interact is evident enough, and it is no secret that they are frequently combined. Yet a distinction must be made. Being poor is often associated with considerable personal qualities; being dependent rarely so. This is not to say that dependent people are not brave, resourceful, admirable, but simply that their situation is never enviable, and rarely admired. It is an incomplete state in life: normal in the child, abnormal in the adult. In a world where complete men and women stand on their own feet, persons who are dependent— as the buried imagery of the word denotes—hang.

It would trifle with the experience of the past twenty years to suggest that we have full confidence in our knowledge of this problem. Yet we have *some*. To restate an earlier proposition, there are things we do seem to have learned, and none more promising than the success of job training for women on AFDC. Thus, the Manpower Demonstration Research Corporation conducted an extended demonstration and research project in the late 1970s on the use of training programs to help hard-to-employ people. For twenty-seven months an experimental group of 1,600 AFDC mothers received jobs, training, and special supervision—"supported work environments"—funded by the

Department of Labor and the Ford Foundation. Their progress was measured against a control group that continued only to get AFDC. The women in the supported work program naturally enough worked more and earned more than the control group during the experiment, but these differences remained significant after the program ended. The program reduced welfare dependency: by the last nine months of the program, participants were twice as likely to have left the welfare rolls as those in the control group. Those who needed the most help made the most gains—older AFDC women (aged 36–44), those with no previous work histories, and those with the longest AFDC histories. (The program was also tried with ex-offenders and young school dropouts. It did not work for them. With former drug addicts, it worked some but not as well as for AFDC mothers. As Mary Jo Bane declares, it is never easy.)

A list of programs for poor women would go on from here. Much is to be done with adoption services—as an example, reimbursing low-income families for the costs of adoption, which can be formidable; or making the costs of adoption tax deductible in much the same way that the costs of having a baby can be deducted as a medical expense.

Much is to be learned about child care and maternity services. In 1985 Dorothy I. Height, president of the National Council of Negro Women, published an article in *Ebony*, "What Must Be Done about Children Having Children." She reports that while early marriage was common in the black community in previous times, and hence early motherhood, "the statistical facts have changed dramatically in one area: Today an overwhelming majority of all

Black children are born to single teen-age mothers." If this is so, it obviously calls for a "mobilization"—Ms. Height's term—to deal with this "crisis." She cites Eleanor Holmes Norton: "It must be regarded as a natural catastrophe in our midst, a threat to the future of Black people without equal."

It is abundantly clear that teenagers in the United States are much more likely to become pregnant than are teenagers in other Western nations. The Alan Guttmacher Institute (1985) reports that the rate of teenage pregnancy among young American women aged 15–19 is 96 per 1,000. In Canada, the rate is 44 per 1,000 young women; the comparable rate in the Netherlands is 14 per 1,000. Moreover, ours is the only developed nation in the world where rates of teenage pregnancy have been increasing of late.[7]

For some time I have wondered whether a reason for the rising rates of teenage pregnancy is the declining age of menarche. This is a large biological change; probably, I wrote in 1973, "the most important event of its kind associated with industrialism. . . ." In round numbers, the age of menarche fell from almost eighteen years in the early part of the nineteenth century to below fifteen years in 1900, and has kept declining. The National Center for Health Statistics has reported that in 1973 the average age of menarche had dropped to thirteen and a half years. Now, a preliminary analysis by the National Center suggests that the age of sexual maturity for young American females has dropped another half year and is now under thirteen years. For the first time, American preteens can have babies. (In 1970 a live birth to a mother aged ten was recorded in

New York City. There are now small but regular numbers of births to twelve- and thirteen-year-olds.) If there is a more pronounced impact of technology on society, I would not know where to locate it. Nor would one expect children to handle it with ease.

A family is formed when a child is born. When an unwed teenager gives birth, a broken family is formed. The National Center reports that in 1983, more than half of the teenage women who had babies were unwed. The result: in 1983 some 261,000 female-headed families formed by teenagers. The number of births to teenagers peaked in the late 1970s, and has declined since. In 1983, one in every five births was out of wedlock. But there has also evidently been a change in mores, for the proportion of births to unwed teenagers has risen. The impact of new forms of venereal disease, such as herpes and AIDS, could yet tighten sexual mores, much as did the advent of syphilis in sixteenth-century Europe. A 1985 study by the Children's Defense Fund states that "marriage is now an almost forgotten institution among black teens. . . . The adolescent single mother was the exception in the black community of the 1950s. Today, she is the rule." Yet again, this condition is becoming general. There are but ten states in the Union where out-of-wedlock births to women under age twenty comprise less than 40 percent of all births; in half the states, this percentage is greater than half. (This for 1982. The range goes from 28 percent in Utah to 71 percent in New Jersey. In the District of Columbia, the number is 88 percent.)

Something is going on here. Years ago, the anthropologist Bronislaw Malinowski laid down one of the very few seemingly universal rules of social behavior, the principle of legitimacy, which holds that every child shall have a recognized father. (Recall that Martin Luther King, Jr., referred to Malinowski's work in his 1965 address at Abbott House.) The biological role of the male human could be that of other species: to impregnate and disappear. "And yet," Malinowski wrote, "in all human societies the father is regarded by tradition as indispensable. The woman has to be married before she is allowed legitimately to conceive. . . . An unmarried mother is under a ban, a fatherless child is a bastard. This is by no means only a European or Christian prejudice; it is the attitude found amongst most barbarous and savage peoples as well." As family makes its way more into public discussion, what might be called the eligible-husband theory has gained some currency. This holds that there are not enough young males capable of assuming a parental role, and attempts have been made to estimate the male-female relation in this regard. Well, yes; but then, no. Malinowski was not describing social customs in economies at or near full employment under conditions of price stability. His assertion is by way of warning and is perhaps best stated by him in *Sex, Culture, and Myth* (1930):

> The most important moral and legal rule concerning the physiological side of kinship is that no child should be brought into the world without a man—and one man at that—assuming the role of sociological father, that is,

guardian and protector, the male link between the child and the rest of the community.

I think that this generalization amounts to a universal sociological law and as such I have called it in some of my previous writings *the principle of legitimacy*. The form which the principle of legitimacy assumes varies according to the laxity or stringency which obtains regarding prenuptial intercourse; according to the value set upon virginity or the contempt for it; according to the ideas held by the natives as to the mechanism of procreation; above all, according as to whether the child is a burden or an asset to its parents. Which means according as to whether the unmarried mother is more attractive because of her offspring or else degraded and ostracized on that account.

Yet through all these variations there runs the rule that the father is indispensable for the full sociological status of the child as well as of its mother, that the group consisting of a woman and her offspring is sociologically incomplete and illegitimate. The father, in other words, is necessary for the full legal status of the family.

(William J. Goode has considered [1960, 1962, 1984] the circumstances in which Malinowski's principle needs to be reformulated, as when alternatives to parental protection are provided. In such a setting, "the principle in fact rests primarily upon the function of status placement, not that of locating a father as 'protector': the bastard daughter of a count is still illegitimate even if he 'protects' her." So equally of the children of welfare?)

Earlier we speculated about the continuing influence of a European view that the "bourgeois family" somehow contributed to the rise of totalitarian regimes. A correlate of that view was the concern of the 1920s and 1930s with the sexual repression associated with societies in which such families were the norm. Anthropologists with reports of the free and healthful sex lives of South Sea Islanders acquired a considerable vogue. This work is now under an evidently successful assault. A careful reading of Malinowski might have avoided considerable confusion. Broadly speaking, he wrote, "freedom of intercourse though not universally is generally prevalent in human societies. Freedom of conception outside marriage is, however, never allowed. . . ."

But we heard what we wanted to hear from the anthropologists, and two generations later the consequences are seemingly upon us. One of these is the emergence of abortion as an issue in national politics. Does this reflect a continuing quest for a "freer" sexuality? Or a belated acknowledgment of Malinowski's hard rule that freedom of conception outside marriage is "never allowed"? These are matters beyond any competence I might have; either way, or by some other causal path altogether, abortion has become an issue of profound and tortured dilemmas.

Each year, 60 of every 1,000 American women under age eighteen have abortions. In Canada the rate is 18 per 1,000; and in the Netherlands, 7 of every 1,000. Fully 40 percent of all pregnancies in American teenagers end in abortion.[8] Abortion is a profoundly serious experience, all the more so for a teenager. The *New York Times* put it recently, "Teen-agers need help to avoid pregnancy, and to avoid abortion." Put another way, should not there be a national effort to protect children from both? In New York City, in 1983, 1,292 girls under fifteen became pregnant, followed by abortions for 988. All this, of course, is part of a larger transformation in reproduction patterns. In 1963, 11 percent of births in New York City were to unmarried women; by 1983 the proportion was 37 percent.[9]

The national policies we have affecting pregnant teenagers, and those at risk of becoming so, are filled with contradictions. In 1970, Congress passed Title X of the Public Health Service Act, providing federal support for family-planning services for those who want them, including poor teenagers. In 1981, Congress enacted another program, providing support for "Adolescent Family Life Projects" to "promote self-discipline and other prudent approaches to the problems of adolescent premarital sexual relations, including adolescent pregnancy." We subsidize family planning services for teenagers while encouraging them not to seek them.

The contradictions are more vivid, and more costly, in the AFDC program. In October 1984, after much urging by the President, Congress established a new "standard filing unit" for the AFDC program. The federal government now requires the states to consider as members of a potential AFDC family everyone, however related, in the household. A new teenage mother who wants to apply for AFDC benefits for her baby and who wants to continue to live with her family must count as her own the income of everyone else in the house; never mind that in giving

birth, she formed a new family, which she now heads. If
the income of the household—the new standard filing unit—
is too high, the teenage mother can move out of the house
and establish her own standard filing unit, and in so doing
presumably qualify for benefits. This is precisely what the
present administration has wanted to discourage. The 1986
budget includes a proposal to terminate AFDC benefits for
unwed minor parents who leave home. The administration
wants to discourage children with children from using
AFDC benefits to establish the financial independence needed
to leave home. Yet, the National Conference of Catholic
Charities (NCCC) points out that "many pregnant girls
cannot remain in the homes of their parents during their
pregnancy for a variety of reasons, sometimes abuse, but
also because of social embarrassment to the parents." The
administration's proposal, the NCCC contends, could have
the unintended effect of promoting abortion as families
who cannot carry the financial burden, or don't want the
pregnancy known, push the young woman toward that
option, inasmuch as others are closed. There are few solutions that can be put in place as regulations. And here
we return to the case-by-case concerns of social work. People and time and money are required, and budget cutting
is not the answer.

Here, however, we begin to touch the limits of government. A credible family policy will insist that responsibility
begins with the individual, then the family, and only then
the community, and in the first instance the smaller and
nearer rather than the greater and more distant community.
In papal encyclicals this is called "the principle of subsid-

iarity." Burke got it plainer when he talked of "the small platoons" of life. This is not a philosophical doctrine, it is a reality principle. In a lecture entitled "Moral Leadership in the Black Community" (1984), Glenn Loury writes, "It is now virtually beyond dispute that many of the problems of contemporary Afro-Americans lie beyond the reach of effective government action and require for their successful resolution actions that can only be undertaken by the black community." This is necessarily so, and so of all groups at all times.

This perception is growing. The tenth-anniversary edition of *The State of Black America*, published in 1985 by the National Urban League, begins with a chapter entitled "The Black Family Today and Tomorrow." Matters are discussed under a series of subheadings: "Pastoral Counseling," "Community Efforts," "Parenting." Only at the very end do we come to "The Role of the Federal Government." A special conference report of the Children's Defense Fund asserts: "If we want all black youth to live up to their capabilities we cannot wait for the larger society to act. . . . The black community has to push society and its youth and itself." In much the same spirit, the Urban League in 1985 began a "Male Responsibility" campaign aimed at young men. "Don't make a baby," stated one of its advertisements, "if you can't be a father." It may be doubted that such admonitions will have the least influence on young men; but it will influence the Urban League, which has had difficulty with this issue to the point of diminishing its once considerable role.

The condition, however, does not abate. In 1980 there

were 468,626 pregnancies among teenage women seventeen years or younger, and 45 percent resulted in live births. In a series of programs conducted from 1980 to 1982, the Manpower Demonstration Research Corporation attempted to "redirect" such teenagers toward self-sufficiency. An array of education, employment, health, parenting, and related services was brought to bear. After one year, the experimental group showed very promising results; but after two years, these had largely disappeared. Barbara Blum reports that "the Project Redirection teens as a whole were doing no better than the comparison group in terms of school enrollment, school completion, or employment. Moreover, about half of each group was again pregnant." In New York, where the corporation is based, teenage mothers with children made up almost a third of the 370,000 families receiving AFDC payments in 1985. If there are to be fewer abortions, there will be more such families. That is about the state of knowledge.

Which brings us to the question of social standards and social pressures. The charge that those who advocate a role for government in social issues ignore the responsibility of the individual is pernicious and wrong, and the record is otherwise. Thus in 1972 Edward N. Costikyan and Maxwell Lehman prepared—for a temporary state commission concerned with the subject—a study on restructuring the government of New York City. To their credit (and somewhat to their cost) they began by proposing that the citizens of New York would have to restructure their sense, as individuals, of what is required of them before much could be expected to come from restructuring government. The citizen, they wrote, is "a governing force himself, ideally exercising some degree of quasi-governmental responsibility around him and his community." Better citizens in other countries, they suggested, have safer, cleaner streets and subways because the citizens there do not regard public property as fair game for destruction.

Asked to provide a formal critique of the study, I began with this central point. The basic fact about New York City, I suggested, was that "its citizens have become less competent as citizens. This has led to the appearance of ever greater incompetence in government." The most important event in the city in recent decades had been the rise of crime, especially violent crime. There was no question that this increase was associated with the rise of heroin addiction to epidemic proportions. Even so, I wrote, "the first fact about a heroin addict is that he or she did not have to become one. It is an act incompatible with competent citizenship." The drug addict was seen as a victim of society, and the contagious nature of the affliction was to be conceded. *"But blaming society doesn't seem to help the drug addicts. Or society. Blaming teaching doesn't seem to help children's learning."* (Emphasis in original.) I see no reason to change those views.

Lawrence M. Mead is currently at work on the question of "obligation in federal social policy," an elusive but essential point, as Costikyan and Lehman insisted in their study of New York. In Mead's view, federal programs—government programs generally—ought to inculcate norms for the public functioning of citizens, and these norms, as regards the essentials of social life must not be permissive where consequent behavior is self-destructive or self-defeating. How this is to be done is the next question, but we never arrive at it unless we ask the first.

There is a possibility, not to be exaggerated and not to be dismissed, of a genuinely punitive reaction to "permissiveness."

In 1985, Dr. Murray published an article in *Commentary* entitled "Helping the Poor." What would happen, he asked, "if there were no provision for AFDC, food stamps, Medicaid, or housing subsidies, but any mother could, if she chose, live with her child in a residential facility? This facility would provide the standard of living and regulation of a good correctional 'halfway house.' . . ." The mind reverts to Jeremy Bentham's lifelong effort to establish the "Panopticon" in Britain, a circular prison of single cells and silent, laboring convicts, all supervised from the center by a private contractor who, as it turns out, was meant to be Bentham himself. Bentham subsequently expanded his scheme to "Panopticon Hill Villages" of portable houses for paupers, orphans, widows, and the elderly, as well as criminals. In this version, the contractor could drag off anyone he considered a pauper. (The contractor would collect revenues from fees charged for a visitors' gallery.) The scheme never came to fruition. Bentham blamed King George III: "But for him all the paupers in the country, as well as all the prisoners in the country, would have been in my hands." All rather zany and quaint from this distance, but dead earnest for Bentham and a good many who supported him at the time. Gertrude Himmelfarb (1968) has related this streak in utilitarianism to the Hobbesian obsession with fear as the animating principle in society. (The proposition Edmund Burke resisted so.) Bentham would go on about "safe and quiet," "peace and calm." The Panopticon, Himmelfarb writes, "like Hobbes' *Leviathan*, was born out of fear. Bentham was not the first prison reformer to discover the virtues of safety and quiet. But he was the first to make absolutes of these virtues, to take refuge in the dungeon as Hobbes had taken refuge in the absolute state." Recall the elders of the capital who in 1969 wanted it occupied by the U.S. Army.

As an alternative strategy, Murray would retain existing welfare programs but commence an active campaign to stigmatize welfare recipients. Rejecting the proposition of the U.S. Catholic Bishops' draft "Pastoral Letter on Social Teaching and the U.S. Economy" (1984) that accepting welfare should not cause feelings of shame, he proposes that receipt of welfare be made positively stigmatizing.

He endorses a proposal of William F. Buckley, Jr.'s, for "taking away the right to vote from anyone who had no source of income except welfare. . . ." Disenfranchisement "would be an official stamp of second-class status: people who live off the largesse of the state should not have a role in determining the rules for dispensing it." This proposal goes back at least as far as John Stuart Mill, an "indirect disciple" of Bentham's, to cite one source. In chapter eight of *Considerations on Representative Government* (1859), he commences his wonderfully meticulous consideration of who deserves the right to vote. Not men of property *per se*, "unless as a temporary makeshift. . . ." And just as assuredly no one without property or income. "I regard it as required by first principles, that the receipt of parish relief should be a peremptory disqualification for the franchise."

Now, of course, Mill was writing in an era in which citizenship was a far more limited concept than it is today. For the record, the Supreme Court in *Goldberg v. Kelly* (1970) held that Mrs. Kelly's eligibility for welfare payments was similar to a property right in the sense that payments could not be withheld until she had received due process of law. J. S. Fuerst and Roy Petty (1985) have commented on the absurdities that can follow such rulings. But let us keep in mind that the provision for dependent children was part of the Social Security Act of 1935. Social Security retirement benefits almost invariably exceed the value of individual and employer contributions. Is this to be considered the receipt of welfare? Are the elderly, then, to be disenfranchised? Or at a minimum stigmatized? It is perhaps not wise to be shocked by proposals intended to shock, but is such playfulness really helpful?

Are there feasible, possibly effective, strategies that do commend themselves? Some. One of the arguments put forth in the 1960s in favor of an "income strategy" to address problems of poverty was the simple administrative fact that the federal government is demonstrably good at redistributing income. Social Security retirement benefits (which redistribute wealth within the older generation, as well as between generations) are the prime example. From there, it is a small step to the thought that the federal government must also be good at collecting income. Which it is, and which in the course of the 1970s it began to do not only on its own behalf but also on behalf of women with dependent children. By 1984, some $2.4 billion was collected under the Child Support Enforcement program for some 647,000 AFDC families and some 547,000 other families entitled to court-ordered support payments. According to an April 1984 Census Bureau survey, nationwide there were 8.7 million mothers with children whose fathers were absent, up from 8.4 million in 1981. About 58 percent of such mothers were awarded or had agreements to receive child support. Total support payments due amounted to $10.1 billion, of which $3 billion was not received because of default or underpayments. If all payments had been made, the Census Bureau estimated that about 80,000 fewer families would have been in poverty.

This is a matter to be pressed *to* the point of punitiveness. If the informal sanctions of society will not enforce the principle of legitimacy, let the state do so. Hunt, hound, harass: the absent father is rarely really absent, especially the teenage father, but merely unwilling or not required to acknowledge his children's presence. The Child Support Enforcement program has the great virtue of paying for itself as well as having the inestimable advantage of linking the issue of welfare dependency to the more general issue of women's entitlements. The national accounts should record progress in this matter or the lack of it. The federal government should have the fullest authority to withhold payments from wages and other income (there is limited but useful authority already). And for the too-much-pitied unemployed teenage male there would be nothing wrong with a federal work program—compulsory when a court has previously ordered him to support his children—with the wages shared between father and mother. This latter is not likely to get started or to work very well if it does. The disorder of the times would likely enough defeat it. But it does make a statement about legitimacy: there must be an acknowledged providing male.

A further advantage of a much-enlarged child-support program is that it brings conservative instincts to bear on a problem that has been too much associated with permissiveness. This precisely was its origin in Congress: "runaway-pappy" measures aimed at welfare families. President Ford, who signed the first such measure, was hesitant. He supported the "objectives" of the legislation but thought the use of the federal courts and the Internal Revenue Service to meet them was "an undesirable and unnecessary intrusion of the Federal government into domestic relations."

We have rehearsed the argument that to the degree there was any societal "decision" about collapsing family structure in the 1970s, it was one of abandonment. The subject grew too difficult, too painful, and attention turned elsewhere. (In Washington this may be noted by the all but total disappearance of the protest organizations that flourished fifteen and twenty years ago. It is difficult to continue protesting when no one pays attention.) Something similar may be observed with respect to drug abuse. To the degree it has returned to, or attained to, the public agenda, this follows from conservative impulses, both personal and political. (As with child-support enforcement, there has been a fortuitous if not altogether happy linkage with another

issue—in this case the discovery by the Reagan administration that Marxist-Leninist regimes could be charged with
complicity in the drug traffic. There is not much evidence,
but if such as there is persuades the current administration
to stop trying to reduce the size of the Customs Service,
all to the good.) It is not clear that the suppression of drug
abuse is something the federal government *can* do, but it
is clear that it is something the federal government must
attempt, and that responsibility surely continues until some
results can be shown.

In this context government responsibilities fall more readily
into place. A federal government that allows its cities to
be flooded with narcotics smuggled past its borders is in
no position to deny responsibility for drug-addicted babies.
Young women don't have to use drugs, and the fiercest
social disapproval is the best hope we have that the present
disaster will diminish. (James Q. Wilson makes the point
that social attitudes toward alcohol abuse had to change
before the problem eased, and it hasn't eased all that much.)
But there would be fewer drug users if there were fewer
drugs. A self-evident proposition is that the federal government should assume as a normal police function the
arrest, prosecution, and punishment of narcotics dealers. It
is elemental. Smuggling drugs into the United States is a
federal offense, and to the degree—the appalling degree—
that even so it is done, the federal government can be said
to have failed to enforce the law. It then follows that the
federal government should be responsible for stopping the
subsequent distribution and sale of narcotics. Federal law
officers; federal prosecutors; federal judges; federal prisons.
The federal government does not now inhibit the use of

drugs to any discernible degree. This should be stated more cautiously: the federal government cannot now demonstrate that it is inhibiting drug abuse. The National Narcotics Intelligence Consumers Committee (curious title) reports that cocaine imports, after declining in 1981, increased 24 percent in 1982 and another 12 percent in 1983. Heroin imports increased in each year. The morgue is the best measure of these matters. In New York City the number of deaths recorded as due to chronic intravenous narcotism, or overdosing, doubled from 1979 to 1984. Control of drug trafficking within the country is left almost wholly to local police, with some help from the states. In 1983 there were 660,000 state and local arrests for drug-related felony and misdemeanor charges as against a mere 14,300 federal arrests, down somewhat from 1982. Is drug abuse to be associated with family issues? Yes, in some direct ways: the children in Hale House. And other indirect ways: the murderous environment around Hale House. A true commitment by the federal government to some definable goal—such as making half the arrests, trying half the cases, imprisoning half the felons—might make a difference. (A quarter of all persons in federal prison are there for drug offenses, but the number is hardly more than five thousand.) An administration committed to reducing the size of government will not do this; but then the notion of family policy extends to denying credit for things not done where family issues are involved. (That does not at all happen at present.) Again, nothing final is to be asserted. So long as drug use is socially accepted, drug abuse will follow. But there are places to begin.

To begin at the beginning can be no great mistake, and

this must be employment. There is no overwhelming proof of this, nor is there likely to be. Yet the proposition commands assent; and here again it is better to trust to social values than to supposed social science. Statistics are a guide. The long downward trend of poverty in male-present families ended in the early 1970s, stayed level, and then rose by a quarter between 1979 and 1983, years of high unemployment. Does this presage a new round of family breakup? Or the *de*feminization of poverty? It hardly matters from the point of view of a family policy that seeks to limit the number of poor children. Employment, especially youth employment, has got to be defined—all over again—as an issue beyond economics. Obviously, at some level of economic abstraction, unemployment rates rising to 50 percent among urban youth are matters of efficiency. Market outcomes can simply be defined as efficient and the matter left there. But where does that leave the nation?

The Congressional Research Service has developed what is, in effect, a serious charge. In 1968 the average income for families in the lowest quintile was 0.91 percent (before taxes) of the poverty level. The top fifth had average incomes 4.18 times the poverty level. This translates into a top group with an average income 4.6 times that of the bottom group. This bespeaks a fairly even income distribution, keeping in mind that income is not fixed through life but rises and then falls with age. The mean annual income of married men with children peaks at about forty-five years of age for those who have completed high school only and at about fifty-five for those with some college. Thus the same families move up in the quintiles, then down. Keep in mind also that the poverty level is a nutrition index: three times the cost of a frugal diet. (We could produce a more sophisticated measure; yet it is useful to keep close to a simple measure based on how much it costs to feed a family.) In 1968 the least well-off families, even so, pretty much *could* feed themselves. By 1979 these ratios had worsened somewhat. The lowest fifth of families had incomes only 0.83 of the poverty level; the highest fifth 4.91; the ratio of one to the other was 5.9. Then came the period of high unemployment noted earlier. The ratio for the lowest fifth dropped to 0.60. (Recall that a ratio of 1.0 means that a family's income equals its poverty threshold.) Every quintile declined in this regard. The top fifth dropped to 4.78. But the ratio of top to bottom increased to 8.0— eight to one. Reaganomics? It is much too early to say; we will know something of that in a decade or so. For the moment it can only be said that those least well-off are of late, absolutely and relatively, even less well-off.

Do the assorted insights we have reviewed suggest that a moderately coherent family policy might emerge as an aspect of national government? A moderately attentive reader would certainly be skeptical. Yet in the abstract, the term *policy* may have an air of authority about it that actual experience rarely confers. I have twice served as an American ambassador—to India and at the United Nations. In that capacity I was charged with carrying out American foreign policy. That there *is* an American foreign policy, endless texts and countless courses attest. Yet up close, try, just try, to get an American President to tell you, his ambassador, just what *is* American policy toward India or at the United Nations. And yet there will be no lack of instructions, no tardiness in assessing success or failure, in ascribing, mostly, blame. The common complaint of the ambassador is that the Department of State does not *have* a policy with respect to the matters with which he or she is charged. Most often, this means that the ambassador does not agree with the policy. But that there needs to be some point of view, some sense of objectives, some assessment of risk, is never questioned. All involved consider foreign policy their business.

Family policy is no one's business at present. The assertion that it ought not to be anyone's business is easily enough defeated in a fair-minded argument. That is, by noting that the policy is at present implicit and that the only question is whether it is to be avowed. It was implicit in the tax code, in the budget, in child-support practices. But being no one's business, for the longest time no one noticed.

Steiner (1981) makes the crucial statement that in the Carter administration "family was unveiled as a major policy area without a theory to explain and guide public intervention." A fair point. Yet experience suggests that policy will emerge, given a conducive institutional setting; perhaps more accurately, policy will be discerned and in some rough way assessed. Does the United States have a trade policy? It has many. Let the secretary of agriculture propose to subsidize farm exports, and the U.S. trade representative soon enough will make a judgment of the policy implications. A civil rights policy? A fiscal policy? An environmental policy? Institutions attend to such matters. Usually several; commonly with conflicting views. But the subject is not simply overlooked; it is somebody's business.

In their paper "Explorations of Family Policy," Sheila B.

Kamerman and Alfred J. Kahn (1976) write, "The real choice is not whether to have a policy but the kind of policy to have. The society may choose a series of fragmented and conflicting family policies or a coherent and consistent one." This is an understandable view, but it is not a working proposition. Such broad agreement might be just feasible in, say, Iceland. It is out of the question in a nation as varied as ours. A. Sidney Johnson, who worked with Walter F. Mondale on the subject of Family Impact statements, responds, sensibly, that the singular "a" along with "national," as in "a national family policy," invites the immediate reaction that "government would seek to impose one single model of family life." Theodora Ooms of Catholic University of America would seem to have it about right in titling an article "The Necessity of a Family Perspective" (1984). It is only in recent years, she writes, "that we have begun to examine closely the nature of the relationship between families and institutions and to ask questions about what effects families have on government and government on families."

To ask questions. There it is. A final example? By the 1970s, the tax code had developed in such ways as to impose a "marriage penalty" on working couples. The mechanism was simple enough. With a progressive tax system, combined husband-wife incomes were taxed at a higher rate than would have been the case were the two paying their taxes as individuals. When the Internal Revenue Service was forced to pass judgment on a couple that was in the habit of divorcing in December and remarrying in January, the Senate Finance Committee took up the subject, but with little cooperation from the Carter administration. In the end, a partial adjustment was incorporated in the 1981 general tax bill. No one in Washington was thinking of taxes in a family perspective and asking questions accordingly.

Ooms notes that the Study Commission on the Family in Britain and the Institute for Family Studies in Australia have provided an institutional setting for such efforts in those countries. She finds no comparable body in the United States, and only the Family Impact Seminar at Catholic University and a center in Minneapolis pursuing the subject independently of government. We can expect more academic centers. Will there be one in government? There was, potentially. The Department of Health, Education, and Welfare brought together the principal government programs affecting families—apart, that is, from tax policy—and was the perfect setting for "a family perspective." Created by President Eisenhower, it was dismantled by President Carter as a reward for support in his 1976 campaign from the National Education Association. Even the honorable term *welfare*, as in to "promote the general welfare" from the Preamble to the Constitution, disappeared, replaced by "Human Services." Still, if a family perspective gains favor, enterprising administrators will provide institutional settings. Similarly, as conservatives take the lead in defining issues from such a perspective, as indeed they have done in Washington in the 1980s, liberals are likely to respond out of the sheer competitiveness of politics.

The prospect that the needs of families might be the means for bringing liberals and conservatives together on matters of policy is intriguing and real.

I am indebted to Nicholas Eberstat for the observation that "liberals" emphasize social policy but are criticized for ignoring values. "Conservatives" emphasize values in the outcomes for children but seem threatened by the idea of social policy. Surely each group is seeing part of the truth and can find common ground in accepting one another's perceptions. Social policy, through the funding of medical research and the provision of medical care, brought about a one-third decline in neonatal mortality rates in the ten years from 1965 to 1975.[10] Social policy can concern itself with the lives of the children who did not die. Let none suppose this a simple matter. Michael Novak points to a further divergence of liberal and conservative approaches. In matters of social policy, liberals don't mind being coercive about matters that affect large groups and classes, but insist on the fullest possible liberties in private lives. If family policy interferes with that, liberals balk. By contrast, conservatives tend to resent the coercions the liberal agenda imposes on large social groups and classes, while thinking of restrictions on family morality as matters of discipline and virtue rather than coercion.

Even so, the promise of the 1980s, such as it may be, is that conservatives and liberals are encountering one another as equals. The long liberal hegemony in the world of social policy has collapsed. (Does anyone recall that in 1947 Lionel Trilling could call for the creation of an opposition within liberalism, to put some pressure on orthodoxy, given the complete collapse of any conservative opposition?) By mid-decade some conservatives were beginning to assert that "poverty" itself was a misleading term—natural only to 1960s liberals who were transfixed by illusory notions that the state could produce abundance and who were indifferent to the proper duty of the state, which is to require virtue of its citizens. From this point, of course, it is not a great distance to the proposition that the virtuous citizen does not permit himself to become poor or that, alternatively, inasmuch as being poor does not preclude being virtuous, it is a matter of no great consequence. We have this sort of analysis degenerate into a genteel social Darwinism or rise to a rugged individualism that is part of our cultural tradition as much as any ethic of collective provision. The central conservative truth is that it is culture, not politics, that determines the success of a society. The central liberal truth is that politics can change a culture and save it from itself. Witness the civil rights legislation of the 1960s that conservatives so opposed.

Nothing warrants optimism. If we turn to the great analysts of our age, we encounter something very like despair.* Urie Bronfenbrenner took the occasion of the year

---

* Although the subject is beyond the scope of these lectures, mention should be made of the work of comparative anthropology of J. D. Unwin, published in 1934 by the Oxford University Press under the title *Sex and Culture*. In a disarming preface he explains that in 1924, "after ten years of intellectual laziness, five spent in war, five in commerce," he decided to devote himself (at Cambridge University) to the study of human affairs.

With care-free open-mindedness I decided to test, by a reference to human records, a somewhat startling conjecture that had been made by the analytical psychologists. This suggestion was that if the social regulations forbid direct satisfaction of the sexual impulses the emotional conflict is expressed in another way, and that what we call "civilization" has always been built up by compulsory sacrifices in the gratification of innate desires.

1984 to note in *Innovator* (September) that Orwell's vision of a war-ravaged world in which the functions of the family were taken over by child-rearing institutions, with the resulting atrophy of close and intimate enduring personal relations, might well be coming true, but not, as Orwell anticipated, because of government interference. "Rather, these changes are the products of governmental and, especially, public indifference. . . . We Americans didn't need any . . . disasters . . . to transform our family life. We did it all on our own. . . ." History, he notes, records in family patterns. But always "the product of some great cataclysmic event: the Huns had come, earthquakes, epidemics, wars, catastrophic economic depressions, or periods of massive oppression. But we Americans didn't need any such disasters to transform our family life. We did it all on our

---

Sixteen civilized and eighty "uncivilized" societies later, he concludes that this is emphatically so. The thesis would today be associated principally with Freud, but Unwin drew on a wide group of theorists and practitioners, the while defending and, to my understanding, quite accurately interpreting the still-controversial Viennese. His unit of measurement, as it might be termed, is "social energy." His conclusion is concise: "In the past . . . the greatest energy has been displayed only by those societies which have reduced their sexual opportunity to a minimum by the adoption of absolute monogamy." There is a hint of ethnocentricity to his conclusions: Athens, Rome, and Britain alone attain to the highest levels of social energy. And yet the work is determinedly nonjudgmental: "No man has yet proved that human energy is a desirable thing." And it is scarcely sentimental: "In every case [of sharp rise in social energy] the women and children were reduced to the level of nonentities, sometimes also to the level of chattels, always to the level of mere appendages of the male estate."

own. . . ." As a basic social proposition he declares, "A child requires public policies and practices that provide opportunity, status, example, encouragement, stability, and above all, time for parenthood, primarily by parents, but also by all adults in the society. And unless you have those external supports, the internal systems can't work. They fail." And fail they do. Such has been "the erosion of the ecology of family life in the United States."

To James S. Coleman (1982), "it would appear that the process of making human beings human is breaking down in American society." The same forces that break apart the household as a productive unit, in an economic sense, have broken it as a unit of redistribution of income. The elderly are looked after by external institutions; increasingly the young. Could it be, he asks, that ours will be the first

---

This never lasts for long, and decline comes quickly; a generation will do. He concedes the possibility of a steady state of high social energy, but on terms he could not easily envisage: "No society has yet succeeded in regulating the relations between the sexes in such a way as to enable sexual opportunity to remain at a minimum for an extended period. The inference I draw from the historical evidence is that, if ever such a result should be desired, the sexes must first be placed on a footing of complete legal equality."

Unwin's work appeared the same year as Evelyn Waugh's *A Handful of Dust*; he got to the British in the nick of time. He would not, I think, concede present-day American society another half generation (a time period he employs) of high social energy, even supposing all that much remains. It is quite beyond my competence to judge the merit of his work, which has a touch of the *encyclopédiste* about it. Still, I much concur with O. R. Johnston (1979) that the way in which his work has been ignored "sometimes seems positively sinister."

species to forget *how* to raise its young? Coleman resists. (Bronfenbrenner resists.) In the Ryerson Lecture at the University of Chicago in 1985 he asserts that "the fundamental assumption on which publicly supported education in the United States is based is wrong for the social structure in which we find ourselves today. Perhaps the school should not be an agent of the state or of the larger society, but an agent of the community of families closest to the child." Diversity attracts him: in "the ghetto and the suburb" schooling should strengthen the norms that those parents hold for their children, "norms that parents often find undercut by intrusions from the larger society." He proposes to reverse the "very" philosophy that now governs our schools, "public and private."

William J. Goode comes closer to an avowed despair than either Bronfenbrenner or Coleman. From Durkheim we have the proposition that no purely contractual society can arise or continue to exist. ("A dust of individuals.") Analysts following Durkheim assert that "a purely individualistic hedonism does not produce enough commitment to the collectivity for many of the needs of society . . . to be met, that the larger system will not work without important inputs from the family, and that if all individuals calculate only what is best for each person personally, then the integration of the society, and even of the economy is likely to falter." Goode has no great expectations: "Although great social events, as well as specific policies, do affect the family, there is no evidence that any serious attempt at manipulating family patterns on a large scale has ever had much success." Indeed there is none. He foresees an enveloping entropy not likely to be reversed.

And the Godkin Lecturer? Well, there is that business about it being darkest before dawn. All he ever hoped was that this matter might rise to the level of public discourse. This seems now to be happening. If it does, the future will be different, at least somewhat different, and possibly better.

A commonplace of political rhetoric has it that the quality of a civilization may be measured by how it cares for its elderly. Just as surely, the future of a society may be forecast by how it cares for its young.

NOTES

THE MOMENT LOST

1. Human Resources Administration, City of New York, *Dependency: An Economic and Social Data Report for New York City* (New York, 1985).
2. Douglas Kiker, "Johnson Spoke for History," *New York Herald Tribune*, June 6, 1965.
3. Tom Wicker, "Johnson View of Negro," *New York Times*, June 6, 1965.
4. Daniel Patrick Moynihan, "Children and Welfare Reform," *Journal of the Institute for Socioeconomic Studies* 6, no. 1 (Spring 1981): p. 8.
5. Arthur J. Norton and Paul C. Glick, "One-Parent Families: A Social and Economic Profile," *Family Relations* 35 (January 1986): p. 16.
6. Mary Jo Bane and David T. Ellwood, *The Dynamics of Children's Living Arrangements*, prepared for the U.S. Department of Health and Human Services (March 1984), p. 26.
7. Glenn C. Loury, "Moral Leadership in the Black Community," in *Black Leadership: Two Lectures in the W. Arthur Lewis Lecture Series* (Princeton, N.J.: Princeton Urban and Regional Research Center, 1984), p. 6.
8. William Julius Wilson and Robert Aponte, "Urban Poverty," *Annual Review of Sociology* 2. Forthcoming.

9. Eleanor Holmes Norton, "Restoring the Traditional Black Family," *New York Times Magazine*, June 2, 1985, p. 93.
10. Ronald Reagan, "Inaugural Address," January 20, 1981.

"IN THE WAR ON POVERTY, POVERTY WON."

1. "Reagan's Concept of America Hurts Party, Packwood Says," *New York Times*, March 22, 1983.
2. Congressional Budget Office, *Poverty among Children* (Washington: GPO, 1984), p. 3.
3. U.S. Bureau of the Census, *Money Income and Poverty Status of Families and Persons in the United States: 1984* (Washington: GPO, 1985), pp. 3, 22.
4. U.S. Bureau of the Census, *Estimates of Poverty Including the Value of Noncash Benefits: 1984*, Technical Paper 55 (Washington, GPO, 1985), pp. 13, 14.
5. U.S. Bureau of the Census, *Money Income and Poverty Status: 1984*, p. 21, 22.
6. Ibid., p. 3.
7. Rudolph G. Penner, data cited in letter to author, January 4, 1985.
8. Emanuel Tobier, *The Changing Face of Poverty: Trends in New York City's Population in Poverty, 1969–1990* (New York: Community Services Society, 1984), p. 7.

COMMON GROUND?

1. Peter Skerry, memorandum to Leslie Lenkowsky, August 17, 1984.
2. Leslie Lenkowsky, "The Hazards of Benevolence," *This World*. Forthcoming.
3. U.S. Bureau of the Census, *Projections of the Number of Households and Families: 1979–1995* (Washington: GPO, 1979); and data provided by Arthur J. Norton, assistant chief, Population Division, U.S. Bureau of the Census.
4. Henry J. Aaron, "Six Questions Still Searching for Answers," *Brookings Review* 3, no. 1 (Fall 1984): p. 12.

5. Frank C. Ballance, "A Built-In Weakness," *New York Times*, July 23, 1980.
6. Aaron, "Six Questions," p. 15.
7. Elise F. Jones et al., "Teenage Pregnancy in Developed Countries: Determinants and Policy Implications," *Family Planning Perspectives* 17, no. 2 (March-April 1985): p. 53.
8. Ibid., p. 54.
9. Bureau of Health Statistics and Analysis, Department of Health, City of New York, *Summary of Vital Statistics 1983* (New York, 1984).
10. Kwang-Sun Lee et al., "Neonatal Mortality: An Analysis of the Recent Improvement in the United States," *American Journal of Public Health* 70, no. 1 (January 1980): p. 15.

INDEX